Quick & Easy Inverter Microwave Cookbook

" Hope you're ready for some of my fastest and tastiest recipes ever. "

Saucy Lemon-Pepper Shrimp
Ready in less than 5 Minutes

Pineapple Upside-Down Cake
Ready in less than 20 Minutes

Easy Roasted Chicken and Veggies
Ready in less than 25 Minutes

Peanut Butter and Jelly Bars
Ready in less than 10 Minutes

This book is from
the kitchen library of

_____

_____

Mr. Food
Quick & Easy Inverter Microwave Cookbook

by
Art Ginsburg
Mr. Food

GEI
Ginsburg
Enterprises
Incorporated

Panasonic ideas for life

Dedicated to

All the busy people
who strive to put a
homemade meal on the
table for their families
night after night.

You are my heroes!

Contents

Introduction

Welcome to the world of Inverter Technology!

You're going to love my fun, new cookbook featuring the Panasonic Inverter Microwave Oven.

Over the years, I have created lots of recipes for my television show, and my many general-cooking books. And after all this time and all these cookbooks, I have to say that this one is absolutely jam-packed with my easiest, most flavorful and fastest recipes ever!

You can feel confident that these recipes will be easy and flavorful because that's what I stand for – I mean, who wants to get all caught up in complicated recipes requiring loads of ingredients? That's why, if my recipe ingredients aren't ones that are already in your refrigerator and pantry, they're readily available in most supermarkets. And as for how fast these recipes are, that's due to the patented Inverter technology from Panasonic.

What's so special about Inverter technology? It not only cooks and heats our food faster, but heats it more evenly – with results more like we get from traditional oven cooking. Here's an example of how ordinary microwave ovens work versus Inverter models: If you set your ordinary microwave to cook at 80% power, it actually cycles on and off, cooking your item at 100% power for 80% of the cooking time. Inverter microwaves, however, would actually cook that food at 80% power for the entire cooking time.

Is there a noticeable difference? Absolutely! Because the ability to cook at lower powers means more even cooking, less splattering, and, when defrosting foods (meats especially), less chance of rubbery edges. It even allows us to bake a cake that not only won't fall, but comes out with an oven-baked texture! Imagine making roasted chicken and vegetables in less than 25 minutes, pork tenderloin in less than 15 minutes, and pineapple upside-down cake in less than 20 minutes!

It may sound too good to be true, but it is! Panasonic Inverter technology makes it possible. And because all the recipes in this book have been triple tested using Inverter technology microwave ovens, each and every one is guaranteed to be easy, fast, and have you saying…"OOH IT'S SO GOOD!!"

Mr. Food

P.S. Please follow my instructions carefully, using the designated pan sizes and cooking at the designated cooking levels to ensure that every recipe comes out just right.

Microwave Cooking Techniques

Microwave cooking means your food is cooked using microwave energy—and that's completely different than preparing food in a conventional oven. Here are some basics for microwave cooking:

Piercing

Foods with nonporous skins must be pierced, scored, or have a strip of skin peeled before cooking to allow steam to escape. Pierce whole eggs, egg yolks and whites, whole potatoes and whole vegetables. Whole apples or new potatoes should have a 1-inch strip of skin peeled off all the way around before cooking. Score sausages and frankfurters.

Browning

Foods cooked in a microwave will not have the same golden brown appearance as foods cooked in a conventional oven unless these foods are cooked in a model with a built-in browning element, in a special browning dish, or the recipe includes instructions for browning. Meats and poultry may be coated with a browning sauce such as Worcestershire sauce, barbecue sauce, or browning-and-seasoning sauce. Generally, to brown meats and poultry, combine a browning sauce with melted butter or margarine and brush on the food before cooking.

To brown quick breads or muffins, use brown sugar in the recipe in place of granulated sugar, or sprinkle the surface with dark spices before baking.

Spacing

Individual foods, such as baked potatoes, cupcakes and appetizers, will cook more evenly if placed in the oven at equal distances from each other. When possible, arrange foods in a circular pattern.

Covering

As with conventional cooking, moisture evaporates during microwave cooking. Casserole lids or plastic wraps are used to create a tighter seal. When using plastic wrap, fold back a part of the wrap from the edge of the dish to allow steam to escape. Loosen or remove plastic wrap as directed by the recipe regarding "stand time."

When removing plastic wrap, as well as any glass lids, remove them away from you and your face to avoid steam burns. Various degrees of moisture retention are also obtained by using wax paper and paper towels. For more information on microwave cookware, see pages 20 to 21.

Timing

A cooking time range is often provided with each microwave recipe. A time range makes up for the differences in food shapes, the thickness of certain foods, and the starting temperature of foods. *Since you don't want to over-cook food, get into the practice of cooking for the minimum cooking time provided, then checking for doneness. If food is undercooked, it's easy to add a minute or two of cooking time. This helps prevent overcooking.*

Stirring

With microwave cooking, distributing heat evenly is very important. Follow recipe directions closely regarding stirring. As a hint, always bring the cooked, outside edges of the food toward the center, and the less-cooked center portions toward the outside for maximum heat distribution.

Turning

At times, microwave energy will concentrate in one area of food. To help ensure even cooking, foods need to be turned. Turn over large foods, such as roasts or turkeys, halfway through cooking.

Rearranging

Remember, with microwave cooking, smaller portions and smaller items such as chicken chunks and shrimp, as well as individual portions or cuts of meats such as hamburgers and chops placed near the edges of the cooking dish, will all cook faster. To help ensure even cooking, once or more during cooking, remove the food and rearrange it by moving the edges toward the center, and moving pieces from the center to the edges of the cooking dish.

Stand Time

It is necessary to allow foods to finish cooking to their centers without overcooking the edges. Since most foods will continue to cook by something called conduction after the microwave oven is turned off, we generally let them "stand" in order to complete their cooking. For example, the internal temperature of meats can rise between 5°F. and 15°F. if allowed to stand (covered) for 10 to 15 minutes. Casseroles and vegetables require less stand time.

Testing for Doneness

The same tests you use for doneness in conventional stovetop and oven cooking apply to microwave cooking:

• Meat is done when fork-tender or cooked to desired doneness.

• Chicken is done when no pink remains and juices run clear.

• Fish is done when it flakes easily with a fork.

• Cake is done when a toothpick or cake tester inserted in the center comes out clean.

Cooked to Perfection

Never guess the doneness of food! To test for doneness, insert a meat thermometer in a thick or dense area away from fat or bone. NEVER leave the thermometer in the food during cooking, unless it is approved for microwave oven use.

Use these temperature and appearance guidelines:

ITEM	TEMPERATURE	VISIBLE APPEARANCE
Beef (Steaks, Roasts)	160°F.	Medium: Pink center
Beef (Steaks, Roasts)	170°F.	Well-Done: No pink, not dry
Chicken, Pieces	170°F.	Juices run clear, no pink remains
Chicken, Whole	175°F.	Juices run clear, no pink remains
Turkey, Whole	180°F.	Juices run clear, no pink remains
Pork (Steaks, Roasts)	160°F.	Slightly pink center
Fish (Fillets, Steaks)	160°F.	Flakes easily
Shrimp	N/A	Bright pink
Leftovers	165°F.	Varies

Microwave Oven Safety

Safety First! Your Inverter oven is a powerful kitchen appliance. It operates differently from a conventional oven, and with a different set of safety rules. Proper cooking depends on the power level used, the time set, and the quantity of food being heated. Be sure to refer to your owner's manual for a complete list of safety guidelines. It won't take long for you to master your Inverter microwave oven, but remember that safe operation is the first step to maximizing its potential!

1. Small Portions

If you cook a smaller portion than recommended for your recipe, yet cook at the time that is recommended for the larger portion, fire could result.

2. Home Canning/Drying Foods/Small Quantities of Foods

Do not use your oven for home canning or sterilizing. Your Inverter oven cannot maintain food at the proper canning temperature. Improperly canned food may spoil and may be dangerous to eat.

Do not dry meats, herbs, fruits or vegetables in your oven. Small quantities of food or foods with low moisture content can dry out, scorch, or catch fire if overheated.

3. Popcorn

Microwave popcorn that pops in its own package is extremely popular. Always be certain to follow the popcorn manufacturers' directions and use a brand suitable for the wattage of your microwave oven.

Caution: Check package weight before using the popcorn key pad and set the oven to the weight indicated on the popcorn package. Otherwise, the popcorn may not pop adequately or the package may ignite and cause a fire. Never leave your oven unattended while making popcorn.

The popcorn bag gets very hot, so always allow to cool before opening. Open the popcorn bag away from your face and body to prevent scalding steam and burns.

4. Deep-Fat Frying

Do not attempt to deep-fat fry in your microwave. Cooking oils may burst into flames, causing damage to the oven and resulting in burns. Microwave utensils may not be able to withstand the temperature of the hot oil, and could shatter or melt.

5. Foods with Nonporous Skins

Foods with nonporous skins such as potatoes, apples, whole eggs, egg yolks and whites, squash and sausages are all examples of food with skins that can trap hot air and prevent heat energy from escaping. These types of foods must first be pierced before microwave cooking to allow steam to escape and prevent them from bursting.

Always use the recommended weight for programmed cooking. Overcooking may cause dehydration and may result in fire.

6. Liquids

Water, coffee, tea and other liquids can be overheated beyond the boiling point, without any visible bubbling when removed from the oven, possibly resulting in sudden boil-overs when the container is disturbed or a utensil is inserted into the liquid. To avoid this, liquids must be stirred before heating in the microwave, and again halfway through heating. See your owner's manual for more information.

7. Glass Tray/Cooking Containers

Cooking containers and utensils can get extremely hot during microwave cooking. Heat is transferred from the hot food to its container as well as the glass tray in your microwave. Use potholders when removing utensils from the oven or when removing lids or plastic wrap covers from cookware to avoid burns.

The glass tray gets very hot during cooking. Allow it to cool before handling, or before placing paper plates, microwave popcorn bags, or other paper products on it for microwave cooking.

Dishes with metallic trim should not be used, or sparks will fly!

8. Paper Towels/Cloths

Do not use paper towels or cloths with a synthetic fiber woven into them. The synthetic fiber may cause the towel to ignite. Carefully monitor your microwave oven whenever using microwave-safe paper towels in it.

9. Browning Dishes/Oven Cooking Bags

Browning dishes or grills are specially designed for microwave cooking only. Always follow instructions provided by the manufacturers of these items. Do not preheat the browning dish for more than 6 minutes.

If an oven-cooking bag is used for microwave cooking, prepare according to package instructions. Do not use a wire twist-tie to fasten the bag, instead use plastic ties, cotton string or a strip cut from the open end of the bag.

10. Thermometers

Microwave-safe thermometers are available for both meat and candy. Do not use a conventional meat thermometer in your microwave oven. Arcing may occur and sparks will fly!

11. Baby Formula/Food

Do not heat baby formula or baby food in the microwave. The glass jar or surface of the food may appear to be only warm while the interior can be so hot that it could burn an infant's mouth or throat.

12. Reheating Pastry Products

When reheating pastry products, thoroughly check temperatures of any fillings before eating. Some foods such as jelly donuts have fillings that heat faster than the surface, making it likely that the filling would be extremely hot, while the surface remains warm to the touch.

13. General Oven Usage Guidelines

Do not use your microwave oven for any reason other than food preparation unless otherwise indicated by a trusted manufacturer. Be certain to follow package directions carefully. Do not leave the oven unattended while in use.

Guide To Microwave Cookware & Utensils

How do you know which dishes and utensils are safe to use in your Panasonic Inverter Microwave Oven? Since microwave ovens are so commonplace nowadays, most dinnerware, utensils and convenience foods indicate right on their packaging if they are microwave-safe.

Generally, containers that absorb microwave energy are not safe for microwave cooking. For instance, any container that contains aluminum or metal can cause sparking during cooking and pose a fire risk! Also, if plastic cookware doesn't conduct heat, it can melt right into your food. If you're not certain about a particular container, don't use it.

For general tips, consult the guide below:

ITEM	MICROWAVE FRIENDLY?	COMMENTS
Browning dish	Yes	Browning dishes are specially designed for microwave cooking only. Generally you should not preheat a browning dish for more than 6 minutes. Always check the instructions and heating chart included with your particular dish.
Dinnerware labeled "Microwave Safe"	Yes	Some dinnerware may state right on it: "Microwave Oven Safe." Always check the manufacturer's use and care instructions that accompany your particular dinnerware.
Disposable polyester paperboard dishes	Yes	Some frozen foods are packaged in these dishes that can be purchased in most grocery stores.
Fast-food carton with metal handle	No	Not for use in microwave ovens.
Glass jars	No	Most glass jars are not heat resistant
Heat-resistant oven glassware & ceramics	Yes	Ideal for microwave cooking and browning.
Metal bakeware	No	Not for use in microwave ovens.
Metal twist-ties	No	Not for use in microwave ovens.
Oven cooking bag	Generally, but check packaging	Follow manufacturer's instructions. Close the bag with the nylon tie provided, a strip cut from the end of the bag, or a piece of cotton string. Do not close with a metal twist-tie. Make six 1/2-inch slits near the closure.
Paper plates & cups	Most types	Use to warm cooked foods and to cook foods that require very short cooking times.
Paper towels & napkins	Most types (See page 19 for more details)	Use to warm rolls and sandwiches.

ITEM	MICROWAVE FRIENDLY?	COMMENTS
Parchment paper	Yes	Use as a cover to prevent splattering in the microwave. Also safe for use in microwave/convection and conventional ovens.
Plastic microwave-safe cookware	Yes	Should be labeled "Suitable for Microwave Heating." Follow manufacturer's instructions for recommended uses.
Plastic reheating & storage containers	Yes, with caution	Some plastic dishes marked "Microwave Safe" are not suitable for cooking foods with high fat or sugar content. The heat from hot foods may cause the plastic to warp.
Melamine	No	This material absorbs microwave energy, making dishes extremely hot.
Plastic foam cups	Yes, with caution	Plastic foam will melt if food reaches a high temperature, so use only to bring foods to a low serving temperature.
Plastic wrap	Yes	Check to be sure package is marked "Suitable for Microwave Heating," but generally suitable for covering food during cooking to retain moisture and prevent splattering.
Straw, wicker, wood	Yes, with caution	Use only for short-term reheating and/or to bring food to a low serving temperature. Note: Wood may dry out and split or crack when used.
Thermometers: Microwave-safe only	Yes	Use only meat and candy thermometers marked "Microwave Safe."
Thermometers: Conventional oven only	No	Not for use in microwave ovens.
Wax paper	Yes	Use as a cover to prevent splattering and to retain moisture in food.

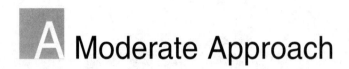

A Moderate Approach

Quick cooking doesn't have to mean throwing sensible eating out the window! Uh uh! Here are a few ways to enjoy healthier eating in less time and without sacrificing flavor:

Chicken

In most recipes, you can substitute boneless, skinless chicken breasts for whole chicken or parts. Remember that boneless breasts are generally thinner, so they'll cook more quickly than bone-in parts; adjust your cooking times accordingly.

Dairy

Look to the supermarket dairy case for reduced-fat, low-fat, and fat-free alternatives. For instance, there's low-fat milk for homemade soups and sauces, instead of heavy cream. (Evaporated skim milk will work, too.) It also works to cut down a bit on the amount of cheese called for in a recipe, especially when it's just sprinkled on top of a salad or casserole, and when using a strong cheese such as Parmesan or Romano.

Eggs

We can replace whole eggs with egg whites in many cases. (Two egg whites equal one whole egg.) And, yes, in most recipes, we can even replace eggs altogether with egg substitute (usually found in the refrigerated section of the supermarket).

Dressings

Add a splash of vinegar or citrus juice – lemon, lime, or orange – to dressings or marinades (and vegetables, poultry, and almost anything else, too) in place of some of the traditional oil. And your Inverter microwave can help you extract that citrus juice with no fuss! Simply microwave a whole lemon, lime, or orange at 100% power for about 20 seconds then squeeze away! Wait 'til you see how much more juice you'll get!

Fish

Fish is a natural fast food that's naturally good for us! And, since all Inverter microwave models have a rotating tray, our fish cooks evenly every time. Just be sure to use fillets or steaks that are all about the same size and thickness.

Meat

- Choose lean cuts of meat and trim away any visible fat before preparing.

- When possible, allow fat to drip away during cooking.

- If cooking ground meat prior to adding to a recipe, after browning, place it in a strainer and rinse it with warm water, then drain and continue as directed to remove most of the excess fat.

Nuts

When a recipe calls for nuts, don't be afraid to cut down the amount. Unless they're being used for bulk in a recipe, we can usually cut the amount by as much as half and still get great flavor and texture. Toasting nuts really brings out more of their natural flavor, so place 1 to 1-1/2 cups *shelled* nuts (shells removed) in a microwave-safe shallow dish coated with nonstick cooking spray. Microwave at 100% power for 2 to 4 minutes, or until lightly browned, stirring occasionally during cooking.

Sauces

There are lots of flavors of prepared sauces available in supermarkets these days, and many manufacturers are offering them in varieties that are lower in calories, fat and/or sodium. These are often thinner than their traditional counterparts, so you may want to use a bit less of them than normal.

Soups

Canned soups are a great beginning for sauces and casseroles. Choosing lighter or reduced-fat or -sodium versions saves us calories while cutting fat and/or sodium.

Vegetables

You always knew vegetables were good for you, but did you know that cooking them in the microwave is not only a quick preparation method, but also a way to help preserve their nutrients and flavor? Go for the veggies!

# Flavor Partners

Want in on the secret to great flavor? It's in pairing the right herbs and spices with your foods. These well-matched combinations are flavors that team well:

FOOD	FLAVORS THAT MATCH
Beef	Basil Black pepper Garlic Red wine Rosemary Soy sauce Thyme
Fish	Basil Black pepper Butter Chives Dill Fennel Lemon Nutmeg Parsley White wine
Lamb	Apple Mint Rosemary Thyme
Pork	Basil Chives Honey Liquid smoke Onion Sage Sweet-and-sour sauce Thyme
Poultry	Black pepper Garlic Italian dressing Lemon Orange marmalade Sage Soy sauce Tarragon
Veal	Basil Black pepper Garlic Lemon Pesto Rosemary Tarragon Thyme

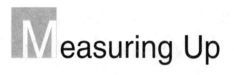# Measuring Up

Keep this chart handy "for good measure"!

Dash	Less than 1/8 teaspoon	
3 teaspoons	1 tablespoon	1/2 fluid ounce
2 tablespoons	1/8 cup	1 fluid ounce
4 tablespoons	1/4 cup	2 fluid ounces
5-1/3 tablespoons	1/3 cup	3 fluid ounces
8 tablespoons	1/2 cup	4 fluid ounces
12 tablespoons	3/4 cup	6 fluid ounces
16 tablespoons	1 cup	8 fluid ounces
1 pint	2 cups	16 fluid ounces
1 quart	4 cups	32 fluid ounces
1/4 pound (1 stick) butter	8 tablespoons	
Juice of 1 lemon	About 3 tablespoons	
Juice of 4 to 6 lemons	1 cup	
Grated peel of 1 lemon	About 1-1/2 teaspoons	
Juice of 1 orange	About 1/2 cup	

Saving Time Means Having More Fun!

Using our Inverter microwaves sure saves us lots of time. So what should we do with all that extra time? Why not get moving and burn some calories...the fun way!

Exercise for 30 Minutes	Approx. Number of Calories Burned
Bicycling (moderate pace)	220
Dancing (slow pace)	100
Dancing (moderate pace)	150
Gardening	260
Golfing (using cart)	120
Playing tennis (singles)	320
Swimming laps	360
Swimming for fun	145
Walking (3.5 mph)	160

Important Note About Oven Wattage

All recipes in this cookbook were tested using a 1300-watt 2.2-cubic-foot Panasonic Inverter Microwave Oven. The wattage and size of your microwave oven affects the cooking times of your recipes. Before preparing any of the recipes in this book, check the wattage and size of your microwave oven* and, if necessary, make adjustments to your microwave cooking times as follows**:

1000 watts: ....Increase cook time by 20%

1100 watts: ....Increase cook time by 10%

1200 watts: ....Make recipes as directed, checking carefully
during each cooking cycle

1300 watts: ....Making recipes as directed, checking carefully
during each cooking cycle

1350 watts: ....Reduce cooking time by 10%

* Oven wattage and size are clearly indicated on your microwave as well as in your owner's manual
** These adjustments are approximate, and your individual experience with various foods and recipes may vary. Be sure to check foods frequently while cooking, and note procedure changes and cooking time adjustments accordingly to assist you when making these recipes again.

A Note About Packaged Foods

Packaged food sizes may vary by brand. Generally, the sizes indicated in these recipes are average sizes. If you can't find the exact package size listed in the ingredients, any package close in size will usually do the trick.

Appetizers

Quick Chicken Fingers
3 to 4 servings

It's amazing! In less than 10 minutes, we have a crowd-pleaser that's perfect for any get-together!

1/3 cup Italian-seasoned
    bread crumbs
1/4 cup grated Parmesan cheese
1/8 teaspoon paprika
2 tablespoons butter
1 pound boneless, skinless
    chicken breasts, cut into
    1-inch strips
Nonstick cooking spray

1 Coat a microwave-safe 9" x 13" baking dish with nonstick cooking spray. In a shallow dish, combine the bread crumbs, cheese, and paprika.

2 Place the butter in a shallow microwave-safe dish and microwave just until melted.

3 Dip each chicken strip in the melted butter, then the bread crumb mixture, coating completely; place in the baking dish.

4 Spray the chicken strips lightly with nonstick cooking spray. Microwave at 80% power for 3 to 4 minutes, or until no pink remains. Serve immediately.

JAZZ IT UP:

Serve these with a variety of dipping sauces, or even individual bowls of warm spaghetti sauce for dipping. They create their own reason for celebration!

Sweet-and-Sour Meatballs
32 meatballs

" This multi-ethnic favorite pairs the sweetness of jelly with the sour of lemon to create fabulous taste excitement. Serve 'em up on a platter with plenty of toothpicks…and it's party time! "

1 pound ground beef
3/4 cup plain bread crumbs
1/2 cup water
1/4 cup coarsely chopped
  fresh parsley
1 egg
1-1/2 teaspoons garlic powder
1 teaspoon salt
1 teaspoon black pepper
1/2 cup grape jelly
1 jar (12 ounces) cocktail sauce
Juice of 1 lemon

1 Coat a microwave-safe 9" x 13" baking dish with nonstick cooking spray.

2 In a large bowl, combine the ground beef, bread crumbs, water, parsley, egg, garlic powder, salt, and pepper; mix well. Form into 32 equal-sized meatballs and place in the baking dish.

3 In a microwave-safe medium-sized bowl, melt the grape jelly at 80% power for 1 to 1-1/2 minutes. Stir in the cocktail sauce and lemon juice then pour over the meatballs.

4 Microwave at 80% power for 7 minutes, or until no pink remains in the meatballs and the juices run clear. Serve.

DID YOU KNOW…

that we can use only certain containers in our microwave ovens? We should not use aluminum or foil products, unglazed pottery, recycled paper, and certain plastics. I recommend sticking with good old tempered glass, ceramic, porcelain, and strong plastics identified by the manufacturer as "Microwave Safe."

Appetizers

Hot Dog & Bean Roll-Up
1 serving

The kids want a fun snack, and we want them to have something they can put together themselves. How do we make everybody happy? Pop these 'puppies' in the micro for an anytime treat in a flash!

One 8- to 10-inch flour tortilla
1/2 cup refried beans
2 tablespoons shredded
    Cheddar cheese
1 hot dog, sliced in half lengthwise

1 Place the tortilla on a microwave-safe plate. Spread the refried beans to the edges of the tortilla. Sprinkle with shredded cheese. Place the hot dog halves on top of the cheese about 3 inches apart. Roll the tortilla jelly-roll style, and place seam side down on the plate.

2 Cover with a paper towel and microwave at 90% power for 1 minute, or until heated through. Slice into small pieces and serve.

DID YOU KNOW...

that the defrost feature of Inverter microwaves allows us to defrost foods more efficiently than ever before? It's perfect for those times when you have to grab some hot dogs out of the freezer.

Pistachio-Stuffed Mushrooms
16 mushrooms

" Want to serve something fancy, without having to search all over town for hard-to-find ingredients? I've got the perfect party-pleaser that's sure to drive your gang nuts! "

16 large mushrooms
   (about 1 pound)
1/2 small onion, minced
1/4 cup pistachios,
   coarsely chopped
6 tablespoons (3/4 stick) butter
1/2 cup plain bread crumbs
2 tablespoons chopped
   fresh parsley
1/4 teaspoon salt
1/4 teaspoon black pepper

1 Coat a microwave-safe 9" x 13" baking dish with nonstick cooking spray.

2 Remove the mushroom stems from the caps, chop finely, and place in a microwave-safe medium-sized bowl. Add the onion, pistachios, and butter; mix well. Microwave at 80% power for 4 minutes, stirring halfway through the cooking time.

3 Add the remaining ingredients except the mushroom caps; mix well. Using a teaspoon, stuff each mushroom cap, pressing down and firmly mounding the stuffing; place in the baking dish.

4 Microwave at 80% power for 4 to 5 minutes, or until the mushrooms are heated through and tender.

DID YOU KNOW...

that these work great even when they're put together in advance? When you know you're gonna be pressed for time, stuff these with the mixture, cover, and refrigerate. Simply heat them just before serving.

Appetizers

Cheesy Broccoli Bites
About 3 dozen

" You know that broccoli cheese soup we all love? Well, I've turned that flavor into a quick-fix, bite-sized appetizer that we can have ready from our Inverter microwave in about five minutes! "

2 packages (10 ounces each)
    frozen chopped broccoli,
    thawed and well drained
2 cups herb stuffing, crushed
1 cup grated Parmesan cheese
5 eggs
1/2 cup milk
1/2 cup (1 stick) butter, cut up
1 small onion, finely chopped

1 In a large bowl, combine the broccoli, stuffing, cheese, eggs, and milk; mix well and set aside.

2 In a microwave-safe 9" x 13" baking dish, combine the butter and onion. Microwave at 90% power for 2-1/2 minutes, or until the onion is tender. Add to the broccoli mixture; mix well.

3 Shape the broccoli mixture into 1-inch balls and place in the baking dish in batches. Microwave each batch at 90% power for 3 to 3-1/2 minutes, or until set. Serve immediately.

DID YOU KNOW...

that when you're steaming broccoli for a healthy side dish go-along, it's best to arrange the florets with the more delicate parts toward the center of the dish? It's the best way to ensure even cooking throughout.

Artichoke Spinach Spread

10 to 12 servings

" This popular appetizer is a favorite in many restaurants that's sure to become a party-pleaser at home! Have plenty of pita wedges and crackers ready, 'cause this one's sure to be a hit. "

1 package (10 ounces) frozen
    chopped spinach, thawed and
    squeezed dry
1 package (8 ounces) cream cheese,
    softened
3/4 cup grated Parmesan cheese
1/4 cup mayonnaise
1 teaspoon fresh lemon juice
1/4 teaspoon ground red pepper
1/4 teaspoon garlic powder
1 can (14 ounces) artichoke hearts,
    drained and chopped

1 In a large bowl, combine all the ingredients; mix well.

2 Spoon the mixture into a microwave-safe 9-inch pie plate. Microwave at 80% power for 3 minutes, or until heated through. Serve immediately.

DID YOU KNOW...

that some Inverter microwaves have a "Keep Warm" setting? If we're not ready to serve a particular dish right away, with the push of a button, that setting helps us keep the food warm and toasty without overcooking it!

Photo at right

Appetizers

Artichoke Spinach Spread
& Dill Crab Dip
Each ready in less than 10 Minutes

Rocky Road Cake

Ready in less than 20 Minutes

Peach Melba Parfaits
Ready in less than 5 Minutes

Marinated Steak Salad
After marinating —
ready in less than 10 Minutes

Dill Crab Dip
10 to 12 servings

" This creamy, dreamy dip is not only packed with flavor, it's a real eye-catcher! I suggest making an extra batch, because this one's bound to go fast! "

2 packages (8 ounces each)
   cream cheese, softened
1/2 pound imitation crabmeat,
   flaked
1 teaspoon lemon juice
1 tablespoon fresh chopped
   dill weed, divided

1 In a medium bowl, combine the cream cheese, crabmeat, lemon juice, and 2 teaspoons dill; mix well then spoon into a microwave-safe 9-inch pie plate.

2 Microwave at 100% power for about 6 minutes. Stir until smooth and creamy. Sprinkle with the remaining 1 teaspoon dill weed. Serve immediately.

DID YOU KNOW...

that there's a simple way to get extra juice out of fresh lemons? Simply heat a lemon at 100% power for about 20 seconds then roll the lemon on the countertop and squeeze away! Talk about getting more for your money!

Photo Page 37

Onion Cheese Dip

About 2-1/2 cups

" This quick-to-fix appetizer saves the day when company's coming at the last minute and we want to make 'em feel special. Let them think you fussed – only you will know the simple truth! **"**

1 medium-sized sweet onion,
   finely chopped
1 cup mayonnaise
1 cup (4 ounces) shredded
   Swiss cheese (see Options)
2 tablespoons chopped
   fresh parsley

1 Coat a microwave-safe medium-sized bowl with nonstick cooking spray. Add the onion and microwave at 80% power for 3 minutes; stir then cook for 2 more minutes, or until the onion is tender. Add the remaining ingredients; mix well.

2 Cover and microwave at 50% power for 3 minutes, or until bubbly and the cheese is melted. Serve immediately.

UNLIMITED OPTIONS:

This recipe is so versatile that you can use almost any shredded cheese in here, from Cheddar and Monterey Jack to mozzarella. Be sure to serve this with plenty of corn chips for dipping.

Appetizers

Game-Day Dip

About 1-1/2 cups

" Looking for a cheesy, gooey dip that's great for game day? Serve this and you'll have a bunch of new fans cheering for you! "

1/2 pound pasteurized prepared cheese product (like Velveeta), cut into 1/2-inch cubes
1/2 cup thick-and-chunky salsa
1/4 cup beer

1 In a microwave-safe medium-sized bowl, combine all the ingredients; mix well.

2 Microwave at 70% power for 2 minutes; stir then microwave for 1 to 2 more minutes, or until smooth and the cheese is melted. Serve immediately.

JAZZ IT UP:

Top with sliced jalapeño peppers and serve with tortilla chips. Remember, this can be as spicy or mild as you like depending on the salsa you use.

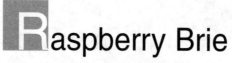aspberry Brie
6 to 8 servings

" It's true that 'we eat with our eyes.' That's why I love to pair one of my favorite varieties of cheese – buttery soft Brie – with raspberry preserves. Not only are they a perfect taste match, but wait 'til you see how colorful and tantalizing this looks! **"**

One 8-ounce Brie cheese round
1/4 cup raspberry preserves
2 tablespoons sliced almonds

1 Place the Brie on a microwave-safe rimmed plate. Spread the preserves over the top.

2 Microwave at 50% power for 2 minutes, until the preserves are melted and the Brie is softened.

3 Sprinkle with the almonds then let sit for 5 minutes before serving.

FINISHING TOUCH: Serve this surrounded by apple and pear slices, and accompanied by sliced French bread and/or crackers.

Appetizers

Speedy Nachos
4 to 6 servings

" Turn your next party into a real fiesta with these colorful starters. They're just as crispy and crunchy as if we'd baked 'em in the oven. Yup, thanks to Inverter technology, we can have that same great taste and texture in a fraction of the time! "

1 can (9 ounces) bean dip
1 can (4 ounces) chopped
   green chilies, undrained
1 package (12.5 ounces)
   tortilla chips
1-1/2 cups (6 ounces) shredded
   Cheddar cheese, divided

1 In a small bowl, combine the bean dip and chopped green chilies; mix well. Place half of the package of tortilla chips on a microwave-safe plate. Spoon half of the bean mixture evenly over the chips and top with half of the shredded cheese.

2 Microwave at 70% power for 1-1/2 to 2 minutes, or until the cheese is melted. Repeat with the remaining chips, dip, and cheese. Serve immediately.

FINISHING TOUCH:

Serve these up with sour cream, salsa, gua-camole, and any of your other favorite go-alongs! Olé!

Potato Nachos

3 to 4 servings

" Looking for a fun alternative to nachos made with tortilla chips? Go with potatoes! These are easy to make, and with so many ways to jazz 'em up, they're a treat with real bite! "

2 large potatoes, unpeeled
   and thinly sliced
1/4 teaspoon salt
1/2 cup salsa
1 cup (4 ounces) shredded
   Cheddar cheese
2 scallions, thinly sliced

1 Arrange the potato slices in a microwave-safe pie plate or shallow baking dish. Season the potato slices with salt and top with the salsa. Cover with plastic wrap, and microwave at 90% power for 5 minutes, or until the potatoes are tender.

2 Sprinkle the potatoes with the cheese and scallions. Cover and microwave at 90% power for 30 to 60 seconds, or until the cheese is melted.

UNLIMITED OPTIONS:

These are perfect all by themselves, or topped with sour cream or ranch dressing.

Appetizers

Crispy Pepperoni Chips

About 4 dozen

“ Not all snack chips are created equal! This one is like having the taste of a warm, oven-fresh pizza in every bite! Don't believe me? Just give 'em a try! ”

1 package (3 ounces)
    sliced pepperoni (see below)
2 tablespoons grated
    Parmesan cheese

1 Place two sheets of paper towels one on top of the other in the microwave oven. Arrange pepperoni slices in a single layer on the paper towels, in batches if necessary. Sprinkle the pepperoni with the cheese.

2 Microwave at 70% power for 1 minute, until the pepperoni is crisp. Let cool, then serve.

PREPARATION TIP:

Use the larger, slicing type of pepperoni to make an even bigger crispy treat!

Anytime Snack Mix

About 10 cups

" I like to put out this crispy, crunchy treat for parties, or any time the gang stops by! "

1/2 cup (1 stick) butter, cut up
1 pouch (1 ounce) onion soup mix
2 cups unsalted peanuts
1 cup oven-toasted wheat cereal
1 cup oven-toasted corn cereal
1 package (6 ounces) fish-shaped
    Cheddar cheese crackers
1 package (5-1/2 ounces)
    fish-shaped pretzels

1 Place the butter in a small microwave-safe bowl. Cover and microwave at 100% power for 40 to 45 seconds, or until melted. Stir in the onion soup mix.

2 In a microwave-safe 4-quart bowl, combine the remaining ingredients; mix well. Add the butter mixture and toss until well coated.

3 Microwave uncovered at 90% power for 4 minutes, or until heated through, stirring twice during cooking. Serve warm, or allow to cool then store in an airtight container until ready to serve.

DID YOU KNOW...

that it's always best to cover foods before heating in the microwave oven? Besides reducing splatters, it helps create more steam which results in faster and more even cooking. Who can argue with that?

Cinnamon-Roasted Nuts

About 3 cups

❝ Who doesn't love the sweet and sinful team of cinnamon and sugar? It's popping up in everything from pretzels to nuts being served up at malls and festivals everywhere you turn! Boy, do I have the easiest, homemade, finger-lickin' treat of them all! ❞

2 cups unsalted mixed nuts
1/2 cup sugar
1 egg white
1 teaspoon ground cinnamon

1 In a microwave-safe 7" x 11" baking dish, combine all the ingredients; mix well to coat the nuts then spread the mixture over the bottom of the baking dish.

2 Microwave at 60% power for 7 minutes, or until crispy. Stir well; let cool.

3 Serve, or store in an airtight container until ready to serve.

DID YOU KNOW...

that we can toast nuts in the Inverter microwave rather than in a conventional thermal oven? Yup, all we do is spread about 1-1/2 cups of *shelled* nuts (shells removed) over the bottom of a microwave-safe pie plate, and microwave at 100% power for 2 to 4 minutes, stirring occasionally, until golden. It couldn't be easier, right?

Breakfast, Brunch & Beverages

Grab-'n'-Go Egg Sandwich
1 serving

" If you're like me, you're someone who's always on the go and needs a quick get-me-going breakfast before heading out the door. This one sure takes less time than sitting in the fast-food drive-through lane, since it uses Panasonic's lightning-fast Inverter technology! "

1 egg
Salt to taste, optional
Pepper to taste, optional
2 tablespoons shredded
    Cheddar cheese
1 English muffin or bagel, split

1 Coat a 2-cup measuring cup or a small round microwave-safe container with nonstick cooking spray.

2 Break the egg into the cup, sprinkle with salt and pepper, if desired, and scramble; stir in the cheese.

3 Microwave at 100% power for 1 minute, or just until set.

4 Meanwhile, toast the English muffin or bagel. Place the cooked egg on the bottom half of the English muffin or bagel; top, and serve.

UNLIMITED OPTIONS:

For a heartier egg sandwich, mix in chunks of cooked ham or brown 'n' serve breakfast sausage, or maybe a sprinkle of bacon bits. Wanna go lighter? Switch it up with a healthy egg substitute (fresh or frozen). Remember: 1/4 cup egg substitute equals one egg.

Breakfast, Brunch & Beverages

Mean & Lean Sausage Scramble

4 servings

" When we're all on the run and there's no time to lose, we can still have a breakfast that'll keep us going all morning long! **"**

1/4 pound bulk Italian turkey
    or pork sausage
1 can (8.75 ounces) whole-kernel
    corn, drained
2 scallions, thinly sliced
5 eggs
1/3 cup fat-free (skim) milk
1/4 teaspoon salt
1/4 teaspoon black pepper

1 Place 2 paper towels in a microwave-safe 9-inch pie plate. Crumble sausage onto the paper towels then cover with an additional paper towel.

2 Microwave the sausage at 90% power for 2 minutes. Remove the paper towels then stir in the corn and scallions; spread the mixture evenly over the bottom of the plate. Microwave at 90% power for 1 minute.

3 In a medium bowl, beat the eggs, milk, salt, and pepper until well combined. Pour over the sausage mixture. Cover with plastic wrap and microwave at 90% power for 2 minutes. Stir, moving the cooked mixture toward the center of the dish. Cover and microwave at 90% power for 2 more minutes.

4 Let stand, covered, for 1 to 2 minutes, or until the eggs are set. Cut into wedges and serve.

JAZZ IT UP:

Add some shredded Cheddar, Muenster, or a favorite cheese blend to the mix.

Cheesy Veggie Frittata
4 servings

❝ If you thought eggs were just for breakfast…think again! This dish is a perfect choice for brunch, lunch, or even a light dinner. And the best part? Say goodbye to messy pots and pans and hello to microwave ease! ❞

2 cups frozen Southern-style hash brown potatoes
1/2 cup sliced fresh mushrooms
1/4 cup chopped red bell pepper
2 scallions, thinly sliced
4 eggs
1/4 cup fat-free (skim) milk
1/2 teaspoon garlic powder
1/4 teaspoon dried basil
1/2 teaspoon salt
1/4 teaspoon black pepper
1/2 cup shredded Monterey Jack cheese

1. Coat a microwave-safe 9-inch pie plate with nonstick cooking spray. Add the potatoes, mushrooms, bell pepper, and scallions. Cover with plastic wrap and microwave at 90% power for 3 minutes, or until the peppers are crisp-tender.

2. In a small bowl, beat the eggs, milk, garlic powder, basil, salt, and black pepper until well blended then pour over the potato mixture. Cover and microwave at 90% power for 1-1/2 to 2 minutes. Stir, pushing the cooked portions to the center of the plate.

3. Cover and microwave at 90% power for 1 to 2 more minutes, or until the eggs are set. Sprinkle with the cheese then cut into wedges and serve.

DID YOU KNOW...

…that practice makes perfect when it comes to making eggs in the microwave? Because eggs set so quickly, you have to keep an eye on them so they don't overcook. Once you get the timing down to cook your eggs just how you like them, you'll be making them in the microwave all the time!

Easy Mexican Omelet

4 servings

" If you love Mexican food, here's a quick take on a veggie omelet that's packed with south-of-the-border excitement! "

4 eggs
1/2 small red bell pepper, diced
1 scallion, thinly sliced
1/4 cup shredded Mexican cheese
  blend
1/4 teaspoon salt
1/4 teaspoon black pepper

1 Coat a microwave-safe 9-inch pie plate with nonstick cooking spray. In a medium bowl, combine all the ingredients; beat until well blended then pour into the pie plate.

2 Microwave at 90% power for 1 minute. Stir, pushing the cooked portions to the center of the plate. Microwave at 90% power for 2 to 3 more minutes, or until set and fluffy. Slice into wedges and serve.

FINISHING TOUCH:

For a bolder taste and look, top each wedge with some salsa and guacamole or sour cream.

Five-Minute Breakfast Sausage
16 patties

" This makes a great go-along for any breakfast sandwich, omelet…you name it! And best of all, it's Southern-inspired and homemade! "

1 pound ground pork
1 teaspoon browning and
    seasoning sauce
2 teaspoons ground sage
1/8 teaspoon ground nutmeg
3/4 teaspoon salt
3/4 teaspoon black pepper

1 Coat a microwave-safe 9" x 13" baking dish with nonstick cooking spray. In a medium bowl, combine all the ingredients; mix well. Form into 16 patties and place in the dish.

2 Microwave at 80% power for 3 to 4 minutes, or until no pink remains in the pork. Serve immediately.

DID YOU KNOW....

that microwave energy cooks food so fast that the fat in the food doesn't usually have enough time to caramelize and brown? That's why, until now, we have traditionally used browning and seasoning sauce to add rich brown color to foods cooked in the microwave. And now there are Inverter models with a browning element!

Impossible Double-Cheese Quiche
6 to 8 servings

" Baking a quiche in our traditional oven can be tough when we only have a small amount of time in the morning before the gang wants breakfast. But with our microwave and fewer than 10 ingredients, we can have a tasty, quick quiche that's far from impossible! "

2 eggs
1 package (8 ounces) cream cheese, softened
2 scallions, thinly sliced
1 cup (4 ounces) shredded Swiss cheese
1 cup (4 ounces) shredded Cheddar cheese
1/2 cup diced deli ham
1/3 cup biscuit baking mix
1 tablespoon Dijon mustard
1/4 teaspoon black pepper

1 Coat a microwave-safe 9-inch pie plate with nonstick cooking spray. In a medium bowl, combine all the ingredients and beat with an electric mixer until well blended. Spread into the plate.

2 Microwave at 70% power for 8 to 9 minutes, or until set. Let sit for 2 minutes then cut into wedges and serve.

DID YOU KNOW...

that we can soften cream cheese in the microwave in no time? Simply unwrap it, place it in a bowl, and, after about 30 seconds in the microwave at 70% power, it's ready to go!

Seven-Minute Cinnamon Buns
6 to 8 servings

❝ The last thing we want to do in the morning is get up and start baking. What if I told you that we could have ooey-gooey, fresh-baked cinnamon buns in under 10 minutes? Well, we can… ❞

1 large package (16.3 ounces) refrigerated buttermilk biscuits (8 biscuits)
1 tablespoon butter, melted
1/4 cup granulated sugar
1 teaspoon ground cinnamon
1/4 cup chopped pecans
1/2 cup confectioners' sugar
4 teaspoons milk

1 Separate the biscuit dough and cut each biscuit into 4 pieces; place the pieces in a large bowl. Pour the melted butter over the biscuit pieces.

2 In a small bowl, combine the granulated sugar, cinnamon, and pecans. Sprinkle the sugar mixture over the dough and toss until evenly coated; transfer the mixture to a microwave-safe 9-inch deep-dish pie plate.

3 Microwave at 70% power for 5 minutes. Remove from the microwave then let cool for 2 minutes; invert onto a serving platter.

4 Meanwhile, in a small bowl, combine the confectioners' sugar and milk to make a glaze; drizzle over the warm cinnamon buns and serve immediately.

Café Mochaccino

6 cups

" If you love the taste of those high-priced gourmet coffees served in trendy coffee shops, wait 'til you starting making them at home! You're gonna be thrilled to see how easy it is, and how much money you'll save by doing it yourself! "

1 tablespoon light brown sugar
6 cups chocolate milk
6 tablespoons instant coffee
   granules
1/2 cup whipped cream

1 Place the brown sugar in a shallow dish. Moisten the rims of 6 coffee cups or mugs with water then dip in brown sugar.

2 In a large microwave-safe bowl, combine the chocolate milk and instant coffee granules. Microwave at 100% power for 10 minutes, or until hot and the coffee granules have dissolved.

3 Pour into the prepared cups then top each with a dollop of whipped cream.

JAZZ IT UP:

This tastes even better served with biscotti or other crisp cookies that just seem made for dunking!

Hot Cocoa Mix
3 cups mix, 12 servings

When there's a chill in the air and you feel like having a soothing, hot cup of cocoa, this mix is just what you'll want to have on hand — whether you'll be enjoying it cuddled up at home or taking it to go!

2 cups nonfat dry milk
3/4 cup sugar
1/2 cup unsweetened cocoa
1/2 cup powdered nondairy creamer
1/8 teaspoon salt

1 In a large bowl, combine all the ingredients; mix well then use as directed below, or store in a tightly covered container until ready to use.

To make a mug of hot chocolate: Microwave 3/4 cup water at 100% power for 1-1/2 minutes, or until boiling. Carefully remove from the microwave and stir in 1/4 cup hot cocoa mix; mix well.

FINISHING TOUCH:

Just before serving, top each mug with a few miniature marshmallows to make it look and taste even more homemade!

Russian Tea

4 to 6 servings

This specialty, known for its orange zing, is great for tea parties. Serve it alongside your favorite tea cookies and finger sandwiches for a taste of true comfort! ❞

2 cups water
2 cups orange juice
2 cups pineapple juice
1/4 cup sugar
2 tea bags
1 lemon, thinly sliced

1 In a large microwave-safe bowl, combine the water, orange juice, pineapple juice, and sugar; mix well. Add the tea bags and microwave at 90% power for 14 to 15 minutes, or until the tea begins to boil.

2 Carefully remove the bowl from the microwave oven. Using a fork, dip the tea bags up and down in the liquid to fully brew the tea. Remove the tea bags and add the lemon slices. Stir then serve.

FINISHING TOUCH:

Garnish each mug with a slice of orange and a sprig of fresh mint. It not only looks great, but it adds a flavor zing!

Breakfast, Brunch & Beverages

Pineapple Wassail

6 to 8 servings

Everybody's sung about or at least heard of wassail — but do you know what it is? It's a steaming hot fruit punch that's always welcoming morning noon, or night. And since now it can be ready in minutes, it's perfect for last-minute get-togethers!

3 cups pineapple juice
1 can (12 ounces) frozen orange
    juice concentrate, thawed
3 cups water
1/2 cup packed light brown sugar
1 teaspoon fresh lemon juice
2 cinnamon sticks
2 whole cloves

1 In a large microwave-safe bowl, combine all the ingredients.

2 Microwave at 100% power for 10 minutes. Stir then microwave at 100% power for 2 more minutes. Ladle into mugs and serve hot.

FINISHING TOUCH:

It's fun to dress this up by garnishing each glass with a spear of fresh pineapple and a maraschino cherry.

Butterscotch Brew

4 to 6 servings

" Want a warm and cozy change-of-pace drink? Well, I've got a sweet solution that's so sinful, it's almost like sipping dessert! *"*

4 cups milk
1 cup butterscotch chips
1/2 cup miniature marshmallows

1 In a medium-sized microwave-safe bowl, combine all the ingredients.

2 Microwave at 70% power for 6 minutes, stirring halfway through the cooking time. Stir then pour into mugs and serve.

DID YOU KNOW...

that it's easy to refresh marshmallows that have gotten hard sitting in your pantry for a long time? Simply place them in a resealable plastic storage bag with 2 to 3 slices of fresh white bread and let stand for 3 days.

Soups & Salads

Tortilla Chicken Soup

5 to 6 servings

Spice up your next chicken soup with the tastes from south of the border! How spicy is it? Well, that's up to you! And whether you prefer your soup mild or spicy, it's a real treat when you want to stay home but still enjoy authentic Mexican flavors!

2 cans (14 ounces each)
    ready-to-use chicken broth
1/2 cup water
1 cup medium or hot salsa
1/2 pound boneless, skinless
    chicken breast, cut into
    1/2-inch chunks
Two 6-inch flour tortillas,
    cut into 3" x 1/4" strips
1/2 cup (2 ounces) finely
    shredded Cheddar cheese
2 scallions, thinly sliced

1. In a microwave-safe 2-quart bowl, combine the chicken broth, water, salsa, and chicken chunks; mix well.

2. Cover and microwave at 90% power for 13 minutes.

3. Remove the soup from the microwave and add the tortilla strips; mix well. Ladle into bowls, sprinkle each serving with cheese and scallions, and serve.

Chinese Chicken Soup

8 to 10 servings

" There's no need to order take-out now that we can create the tastes of the Orient right in our own kitchens! And when the gang finishes cleaning their plates, why not bring out some fortune cookies to complete their dining experience! "

3 cans (14 ounces each)
    ready-to-use chicken broth
3/4 cup water
2 tablespoons soy sauce
1 cup sliced mushrooms
1 can (8 ounces) sliced
    water chestnuts, drained
1 can (8 ounces) sliced
    bamboo shoots, drained
1/2 pound boneless, skinless
    chicken breast,
    cut into 1/2-inch chunks
1/4 pound uncooked spaghetti,
    broken into pieces
2 scallions, thinly sliced

1 In a microwave-safe 4-quart bowl, combine all the ingredients except the scallions.

2 Microwave at 90% power for 20 to 22 minutes, stirring occasionally until the spaghetti is tender and no pink remains in the chicken.

3 Sprinkle the soup with scallions, ladle into bowls, and serve.

DID YOU KNOW...

that microwaves only heat food to a depth of about 2 inches? That means that it's important to stir deeper, denser foods frequently while cooking, to make sure they heat all the way through.

Soups & Salads

Hearty Hamburger Soup
8 to 10 servings

" It's amazing! We can turn ordinary hamburger into one extraordinary soup! Whether we fill the kids' thermoses with it, or serve up dinnertime fun, this is one soup they'll never forget! "

1 pound ground beef
1 medium onion, chopped
3 cans (14 ounces each)
    ready-to-use beef broth
1 can (15 ounces) crushed tomatoes
1 package (16 ounces) frozen
    peas and carrots
1 teaspoon salt
1 teaspoon black pepper

1 In a microwave-safe 4-quart bowl, cook the ground beef and onion at 80% power for 4 to 5 minutes, until no pink remains in the meat, stirring halfway through the cooking to break up any meat chunks; drain.

2 Stir in the remaining ingredients then microwave at 80% power for 14 to 15 minutes, or until the soup is hot. Ladle into bowls and serve.

UNLIMITED OPTIONS:

Mix this up as directed, or vary it each time you make it by adding your favorite frozen or canned veggies – potatoes, beans, squash… you name it! Make it a little heartier, a little lighter – it's up to you.

Manhattan Clam Chowder

5 to 6 servings

" I used to think the microwave was good for heating up canned soups from the supermarket – but never thought of using it to make homemade soup! Well, that was before. Now I'm a believer! "

2 slices bacon, minced
1 celery rib, finely chopped
1 medium carrot, finely chopped
1 medium onion, finely chopped
2 medium potatoes, peeled and diced
1 can (14-1/2 ounces) diced
    tomatoes, undrained
1 bottle (8 ounces) clam juice
2 tablespoons tomato paste
1 teaspoon dried thyme
2 cans (6-1/2 ounces each)
    chopped clams, undrained

1 Place the bacon in a microwave-safe 3-quart bowl. Cover and microwave at 80% power for 2 minutes, or until crisp.

2 Add the remaining ingredients except the chopped clams; mix well. Cover, and microwave at 80% power for 14 minutes, or until the vegetables are tender.

3 Stir in the clams then microwave at 80% power for 1 to 2 minutes, or until heated through. Ladle into bowls and serve.

FINISHING TOUCH: Serve this hearty soup with a sprinkle of Parmesan cheese and a slice of crusty Italian bread for dunking.

Veggie Patch Soup

7 to 8 servings

At the touch of a button, you'll be enjoying this farm-fresh soup that's chock-full of healthy, good-for-you veggies, and tastes like it's been simmering all day!

3 cans (14 ounces each)
    ready-to-use vegetable broth
1 medium onion, finely chopped
1 cup shredded cabbage
2 medium carrots, cut into thin slices
1/2 teaspoon dried thyme
2 medium zucchini, cut into
    1/2-inch chunks
1 can (14-1/2 ounces) whole
    potatoes, drained and
    cut into 1/2-inch chunks
1 tomato, chopped
1/4 teaspoon black pepper

1 In a microwave-safe 4-quart bowl, combine the vegetable broth, onion, cabbage, carrots, and thyme. Cover and microwave at 100% power for 15 minutes.

2 Add the zucchini, potatoes, tomato, and pepper to the bowl. Cover and microwave at 100% power for 9 minutes, or until the vegetables are tender. Ladle into bowls and serve.

Cheesy Potato Soup

4 to 5 servings

" A meal in itself, this rich and hearty soup is sure to become a household favorite! It's amazing how fast we can go from kitchen to dining room with this 'souper' soup! "

2 cans (14 ounces each)
    ready-to-use chicken broth
1 cup half-and-half
1 cup instant mashed potato flakes
2 cups (8 ounces) finely shredded
    sharp Cheddar cheese
1/4 teaspoon black pepper
1 scallion, thinly sliced (optional)

1 In a microwave-safe 3-quart bowl, combine the chicken broth and half-and-half; mix well. Microwave at 100% power for 6 minutes, or until bubbly.

2 Stir in the remaining ingredients except the scallion, if desired, and microwave at 80% power for 3 minutes, or until the mixture is thickened and the cheese is melted. Ladle into bowls, top with scallion rings, if desired, and serve.

FINISHING TOUCH:

To fancy this up, sprinkle each serving with a bit of shredded Cheddar cheese and a generous dose of bacon bits just before serving.

Very Garlic Soup

5 to 6 servings

" Garlic-lovers, do I have the dish for you! Yes, eight garlic cloves may sound like a lot but, I promise you, one taste of this golden classic and it's sure to be a hit! "

1 teaspoon olive oil
8 garlic cloves, minced
2 cans (14 ounces each)
    ready-to-use chicken broth
1 cup water
1/4 teaspoon black pepper
1 egg, beaten
3 slices toasted bread,
    cut into 1/2-inch cubes
1 scallion, thinly sliced

1 In a microwave-safe 4-quart bowl, combine the olive oil and garlic. Microwave at 90% power for 2 minutes, or until the garlic is tender.

2 Add the chicken broth, water, and pepper; mix well. Cover and microwave at 90% power for 5 minutes.

3 Remove 2 tablespoons of the soup to a small bowl, and combine with the beaten egg. Pour the egg mixture into the soup and stir with a fork.

4 Cover and microwave at 90% power for 2 minutes, or until heated through. Stir in the toast cubes and scallions. Ladle into bowls and serve.

DID YOU KNOW...

that the health benefits of garlic have been recognized for over 2,000 years? It's been shown to be a great antioxidant and helpful in managing cardiovascular health... and it makes everything taste great too!

Rich & Creamy Corn Chowder

4 to 5 servings

“ We want our families to get their five-a-day servings of fruit and vegetables, and this one sure helps us get there…deliciously! ”

2 cans (14-3/4 ounces each)
    cream-style corn
1-2/3 cups milk
2 tablespoons butter
1/4 teaspoon salt
1/4 teaspoon black pepper

1 In a microwave-safe 3-quart bowl, combine all the ingredients; mix well.

2 Microwave at 90% power for 7 minutes, or until heated through. Ladle into bowls and serve.

FINISHING TOUCH:

Give this soup a grand finale by topping off each serving with a dollop of sour cream and a sprig of fresh cilantro.

Zippy Black Bean Soup

5 to 6 servings

" This soup's just the thing when you want to surprise 'em with something that'll make their taste buds go wild! "

1 small onion, finely chopped
2 cans (15 ounces) black beans,
    undrained
1 can (14 ounces)
    ready-to-use chicken broth
1 cup salsa
1 teaspoon ground cumin

1 Place the onion in a large microwave-safe bowl. Cover and microwave at 100% power for 2 minutes, or until the onion is tender.

2 In a blender, purée one can of black beans with its liquid until smooth. Add to the onions along with the remaining can of undrained beans. Add the chicken broth, salsa, and cumin; mix well.

3 Cover and microwave at 100% power for 10 minutes, or until heated through and the beans are tender. Ladle into bowls and serve.

FINISHING TOUCH:

Add color and freshness by garnishing each serving with a dollop of sour cream and a wedge of lime.

Marinated Steak Salad

4 to 6 servings

" Just wait 'til you see your gang's reaction when you bring this to the dinner table! Better yet, watch their faces when you tell them you cooked it in the microwave! You'll have to agree with me that the Panasonic Inverter Microwave is not just *any* microwave! **"**

1/4 cup olive oil
Juice of 1 lime
1 small onion, minced
1 tablespoon crushed red pepper
1 teaspoon salt
One 1-pound beef flank steak
1/2 cup mayonnaise
1/2 cup chili sauce
1 head romaine lettuce,
    cut into bite-sized pieces
1 can (2.25 ounces)
    sliced olives, drained
1 package (4 ounces) crumbled
    feta cheese

1 In a microwave-safe 7" x 11" baking dish, combine the oil, lime juice, onion, crushed red pepper, and salt; mix well. Add the steak and turn to coat. Cover and marinate in the refrigerator for at least 4 hours, turning occasionally.

2 In a small bowl, combine the mayonnaise and chili sauce; whisk until well combined then cover and chill.

3 Drain and discard the marinade from the steak. Microwave at 100% power for 4 to 5 minutes, or until desired doneness. Slice the steak thinly across the grain.

4 Place the lettuce on a serving platter and arrange the steak slices over it. Sprinkle with the olives and feta cheese then drizzle with the chilled mayonnaise mixture. Serve immediately.

UNLIMITED OPTIONS:

To save even more time, marinate the steak the night before you plan to serve it. Then, when you're ready, simply cook the marinated meat and prepare the salad. Serve it up with a slice of crusty, Italian bread for a complete meal in no time!

Photo Page 40

Spinach Salad with Hot Bacon Dressing

4 to 6 servings

" You might remember seeing this on fancy restaurant menus. It's a nice change of pace from the same old everyday salad. Why, not only does it make a great go-along for dinner, but it's a zippy lunch all by itself! "

8 slices bacon, chopped
1/4 cup apple cider vinegar
2 teaspoons fresh lemon juice
2 tablespoons sugar
1/4 teaspoon black pepper
1 package (10 ounces) fresh
    spinach, washed and trimmed
1 hard-boiled egg, chopped

1 Place the bacon in a medium-sized microwave-safe bowl and microwave at 80% power for 5 to 6 minutes, until the bacon is crisp, stirring halfway through the cooking.

2 Add the vinegar, lemon juice, sugar, and pepper; mix well. Place the spinach in a serving bowl, add the hot bacon dressing, and toss to coat. Sprinkle with egg and serve immediately.

DID YOU KNOW...

that we can use our Inverter microwaves to separate frozen bacon? Simply remove the wrapper and place the bacon in a microwave-safe dish. Microwave on high (Power Level 10) for about 30 seconds then separate the slices with a spatula.

Warm Honey-Walnut Salad
4 to 6 servings

" Wow! Say goodbye to ho-hum salads, 'cause this is one honey of a treat! Wait 'til you taste this sweet and tangy homemade dressing – you'll want to put it on everything from salads to poultry and more! "

1/4 cup Italian salad dressing
3 tablespoons honey
2 tablespoons maple syrup
1 tablespoon peanut oil
2 tablespoons chopped walnuts
1 package (8 ounces) mixed
    baby greens

1 Place all the ingredients except the mixed baby greens in a medium-sized microwave-safe bowl.

2 Microwave at 100% power for 1-1/2 minutes, or until warm; stir until well combined.

3 Toss the dressing with the mixed greens, and serve.

FINISHING TOUCH:

This looks really great garnished with additional walnut halves, orange slices, and red onion rings. It even works great if you want to hearty it up with chunks of cooked chicken or ham.

Hot Bacon 'n' Potato Salad

6 to 8 servings

" Think this is a plain-old potato salad recipe? Think again! The crisp cooked bacon mixed with these tender potatoes can turn any old backyard barbecue into a reason to celebrate! "

1/2 pound bacon

1-1/2 pounds small red creamer potatoes, washed and thinly sliced

2 cups water

1 teaspoon salt

1 cup mayonnaise

3 tablespoons sugar

2 tablespoons apple cider vinegar

1/4 teaspoon black pepper

1 Place the bacon slices between layers of paper towels. Microwave at 80% power for 7 minutes; let cool.

2 Place the potatoes, water, and salt in a large microwave-safe bowl. Cover and microwave at 100% power for 12 to 13 minutes, or until tender; drain.

3 Crumble the bacon over the potatoes and add the remaining ingredients; mix well. Serve warm.

DID YOU KNOW...

that the skin of whole potatoes must be pierced a few times with a fork or knife before baking or microwaving? Doing this keeps the steam from building up inside the potatoes and causing them to burst!

Scrambled Egg Salad

3 to 4 servings

" When we're scrambling to get lunches made and everybody out the door in the morning, what could be better than a quick 'n' creamy egg salad? It's perfect for packing in the kids' lunch boxes and even having on hand for a nourishing snack! "

6 eggs
1/3 cup mayonnaise
1/2 teaspoon yellow mustard
1/4 teaspoon salt
1/8 teaspoon black pepper

1 Break the eggs into a microwave-safe pie plate; mix just until the yolks and whites are combined.

2 Microwave at 100% power for 1-1/2 to 2 minutes, or until the eggs start to set around the edges; push the edges to the center. Repeat at 30-second intervals, until the eggs are just set.

3 Allow to cool then chop finely. Add the mayonnaise, mustard, salt, and pepper; mix well. Serve, or cover and chill until ready to serve.

DID YOU KNOW...

that it's not yet possible to make hard-boiled eggs in the microwave oven? If you're a fan of hard-boiled eggs, like me, you're gonna have to stick to boiling them on the stovetop for now. That's because, if you were to heat an egg in its shell in the microwave, the steam could get underneath the shell and cause the egg to explode. That's *not* the way to save time in the kitchen!

Main Courses

Main Courses, continued

Fish & Seafood

Meatless Entrées

Easy Roasted Chicken and Veggies

4 to 5 servings

" Roasting an entire chicken in a conventional oven takes hours! But with Inverter technology, we don't have to miss out on that great taste because we're short on time. Now we can use our microwaves to give us winning homestyle roasted chicken any night of the week! "

1 teaspoon paprika
1 teaspoon onion powder
1 teaspoon garlic powder
1 teaspoon salt
1/2 teaspoon black pepper
4 medium potatoes, peeled
    and cut into 1-inch chunks
2 ribs celery, cut into 1-inch chunks
2 carrots, peeled and
    cut into 1-inch chunks
1 onion, cut into 1-inch chunks
One 3- to 3-1/2-pound chicken
1 teaspoon browning
    and seasoning sauce

JAZZ IT UP!

Serve this tender, juicy chicken with your favorite quick stuffing and tossed greens for a complete homestyle meal in less than 30 minutes!

Photo Page 3

1 In a small bowl, combine the paprika, onion powder, garlic powder, salt, and pepper. In a large bowl, combine the potatoes, celery, carrots, and onion. Add half of the seasoning mixture and toss until the vegetables are thoroughly coated.

2 Place the chicken in a microwave-safe 9" x 13" baking dish. Brush the chicken with the browning and seasoning sauce, then sprinkle with the remaining seasoning mixture. Arrange the vegetables around the chicken.

3 Cover and microwave at 90% power for 18 to 22 minutes, or until no pink remains in the chicken and the vegetables are tender. Let chicken sit for 5 minutes before slicing and serving.

Quick Barbecued Chicken
4 servings

" When it comes to barbecued chicken, everybody has a favorite. Here's how to satisfy them all with a basic chicken and three great sauces they can choose from. Slather away! "

One 3- to 4-pound chicken,
    cut into eight pieces
1/2 teaspoon salt
1/4 teaspoon black pepper
Barbecue sauce
    [see recipes on opposite page]

1 Preheat the grill to medium-high heat.

2 Meanwhile, place the chicken in a microwave-safe 9" x 13" baking dish and season with the salt and pepper. Cover and microwave at 80% power for 8 minutes.

3 Select and prepare one or more barbecue sauce recipes from opposite page.

4 Place the chicken on the grill and baste with barbecue sauce; cook for 3 to 4 minutes per side, or until no pink remains in the chicken and its juices run clear, basting frequently with the remaining sauce.

PREPARATION TIP:

Although this recipe calls for firing up the grill to finish cooking the chicken and give it that rich, barbecued flavor, we use the Inverter microwave to partially cook the chicken first, saving us both time and effort. And we all know how helpful that is!

Speedy Barbecue Sauces

Traditional Barbecue Sauce
About 1-1/2 cups

2/3 cup ketchup
1/2 cup soy sauce
1/2 cup packed light brown sugar
3 garlic cloves, minced
1/2 teaspoon ground ginger

1 In a large bowl, combine all the ingredients.

2 Baste chicken as directed in step 4 of Quick Barbecued Chicken.

Bourbon Barbecue Sauce
About 1-1/4 cups

1 small onion, finely chopped
1/2 cup Dijon-style mustard
1/2 cup packed dark brown sugar
1/4 cup bourbon
2 teaspoons Worcestershire sauce
1/2 teaspoon salt

1 Place all the ingredients in a medium-sized microwave-safe bowl. Microwave at 60% power for 2 to 3 minutes, or until the sauce thickens and the onion is tender, stirring halfway through the cooking time.

2 Baste as directed in step 4 of Quick Barbecued Chicken.

Sweet Mustard Barbecue Sauce
About 1-3/4 cups

1/2 cup dark corn syrup
1/2 cup ketchup
1/2 cup yellow mustard
1/4 cup white vinegar

1 Place all the ingredients in a medium-sized microwave-safe bowl. Microwave at 60% power for 1 minute, or until heated through, stirring halfway through the cooking time.

2 Baste as directed in step 4 of Quick Barbecued Chicken.

Quick-as-a-Wink Pesto Chicken

4 servings

" With everyone's busy schedules, it's hard to come up with fabulous dinners night after night. But if you have ten minutes and a few ingredients, here's an elegant option sure to become a regular! "

4 boneless, skinless
    chicken breast halves
    (1 to 1-1/4 pounds total)
1/4 teaspoon salt
1/8 teaspoon black pepper
1/2 cup prepared pesto sauce
4 slices (4 ounces total)
    mozzarella cheese
1 can (2.25 ounces) sliced
    black olives,
    drained (optional)

1 Place the chicken breast halves on a microwave-safe platter. Season with the salt and pepper then cover with a single layer of thick paper towels. Microwave at 90% power for 5 minutes.

2 Uncover the chicken and top each piece with a dollop of pesto sauce and one slice of mozzarella cheese.

3 Microwave at 90% power for 2 minutes, or until no pink remains in the chicken and the cheese is melted. Sprinkle with sliced olives, if desired, and serve immediately.

FINISHING TOUCH:

To really turn this into a show-stoppin' dinner, top each serving with a slice or two of plum tomato and a sprig of fresh basil. Mmm mmm!

Fancy Fast Greek Chicken

4 servings

Bring the flavor of the Greek Isles to your kitchen with this family favorite. There's no passport needed for this taste adventure – just a healthy appetite, and a knife and fork!

4 boneless, skinless
    chicken breast halves
    (1 to 1-1/4 pounds total)
1/2 teaspoon paprika
1/2 teaspoon salt
1 jar (12 ounces) chicken gravy
1-1/2 teaspoons fresh lemon juice
1/4 cup dry white wine
1-1/2 teaspoons dried oregano

1. Coat a microwave-safe 9" x 13" baking dish with nonstick cooking spray; place the chicken in the dish and season with the paprika and salt.

2. Microwave the chicken at 90% power for 3 minutes.

3. In a medium bowl, combine the remaining ingredients and pour over the chicken. Microwave at 90% power for 3 minutes, or until no pink remains in the chicken.

FINISHING TOUCH:

To give this fancy chicken even more authentic Greek flavor, sprinkle each serving with crumbled feta cheese and top with sliced black olives!

Jerk Chicken

4 servings

" This flavorful dish, which originated in the Caribbean, is made with a make-your-own jerk seasoning that really packs a punch! This super seasoning works great on both chicken and pork, so give 'em both a try! "

1/3 cup red wine vinegar
1 tablespoon olive oil
2 tablespoons light brown sugar
5 scallions, thinly sliced
2 teaspoons hot pepper sauce
1-1/4 teaspoons allspice
1 teaspoon dried thyme
1/2 teaspoon salt
1/2 teaspoon black pepper
4 boneless, skinless
    chicken breast halves
    (about 1-1/4 pounds total)

1 In a medium bowl, combine all the ingredients except the chicken; mix well. Add the chicken and marinate in the refrigerator for at least 2 hours.

2 Coat a microwave-safe 9" x 13" baking dish with nonstick cooking spray. Add the chicken, discarding the marinade.

3 Microwave at 80% power for 6 to 7 minutes, or until no pink remains in the chicken.

UNLIMITED OPTIONS:

Jerk seasoning blends start with the same basic ingredients, but can be varied from there, depending on what we're in the mood for. Don't be afraid to add a different spice now and then, such as cinnamon, ginger, cloves, or even chili powder for extra kick.

Sesame Chicken Fingers

6 servings

" Whether you're a little kid or a kid at heart, you're gonna love these tender, juicy chicken strips. As an after-school snack or a family dinner, they're great for the whole gang! "

1/2 cup all-purpose flour
2 eggs, beaten
3/4 cup Italian-seasoned bread crumbs
1/3 cup sesame seeds
2 teaspoons dried thyme
1 teaspoon garlic powder
1/2 teaspoon salt
1/4 teaspoon black pepper
1-1/2 pounds boneless,
    skinless chicken breasts,
    cut into 1-inch strips
Nonstick cooking spray

DID YOU KNOW...

you can toast sesame seeds in the Inverter microwave? Toasting them brings out even more flavor, so just place 1/4 cup of the seeds in a microwave-safe bowl and heat at 100% power for 2 to 2-1/2 minutes, stirring twice during heating.

1 Coat a microwave-safe 9" x 13" baking dish with nonstick cooking spray. Place the flour in a shallow dish. Place the beaten egg in another shallow dish. In a third shallow dish, combine the bread crumbs, sesame seeds, thyme, garlic powder, salt, and pepper; mix well.

2 Coat the chicken with the flour then dip in the beaten egg and coat with the bread crumb mixture, covering completely.

3 Place the chicken strips in the baking dish and spray lightly with cooking spray.

4 Microwave at 80% power for 6 minutes, or until no pink remains and the juices run clear.

Honey–Barbecued Chicken

3 to 4 servings

" Who can resist the taste of honey? Not me! And I'll bet it'll have your gang buzzin' when you serve up this honey of a dish! "

One 3- to 4-pound chicken,
   cut into eight pieces
1 cup barbecue sauce
1 cup honey
1/2 teaspoon salt
1/2 teaspoon pepper

1 Preheat the grill to medium heat. Coat a microwave-safe 9" x 13" baking dish with nonstick cooking spray.

2 Place the chicken pieces in the baking dish and microwave at 80% power for 10 minutes.

3 In a small bowl, combine the remaining ingredients; mix well then set aside half of the honey-barbecue sauce. Brush the other half of the sauce over the chicken then grill it for 5 minutes. Turn the chicken, brushing again with the sauce, and grill for 5 minutes, or until no pink remains and the juices run clear. Serve topped with the reserved honey-barbecue sauce.

DID YOU KNOW...

that honey caramelizes at a high temperature? Make sure your grill fire isn't too hot, or the honey in the sauce will caramelize and burn the outside of the chicken.

Chicken Parmesan Bake

6 servings

" I know this recipe sounds so basic that you're probably wondering how good it could be. Well, go ahead and try it…and see for yourself! "

1 jar (26 ounces) spaghetti sauce
1 pound frozen chicken nuggets
1 package (10 ounces)
    frozen chopped spinach,
    thawed and squeezed dry
1 cup (4 ounces) shredded
    mozzarella cheese

1 Spread half of the spaghetti sauce over the bottom of a microwave-safe 9" x 13" baking dish. Layer the nuggets evenly over the sauce then sprinkle with the spinach. Pour the remaining spaghetti sauce over the spinach.

2 Microwave at 90% power for 4 minutes. Sprinkle with the cheese and microwave for 2 minutes, or until heated through and the cheese is melted.

GREAT GO-ALONG: All we need now is a big garden salad and a loaf of hot, crusty Italian bread to get your gang yelling, "Ah é molto bene!!" (That's Italian for "OOH IT'S SO GOOD!!®")

American Chicken Chow Mein
4 to 5 servings

" This Asian-inspired classic was all the rage in the '60s – and will be popular at your house again when you find out how quickly it all cooks up in the microwave, and everybody else tells you how good it is! Here's to the classics! "

2 tablespoons butter, cut up
1 small onion, finely chopped
3 ribs celery, thinly sliced
1/2 pound sliced fresh mushrooms
1 jar (12 ounces) chicken gravy
1 can (10 ounces) chunk
     chicken, drained and flaked
1 can (14 ounces)
     bean sprouts, drained
1 jar (2 ounces) chopped
     pimientos, drained
1 tablespoon soy sauce

1 In a large microwave-safe bowl, combine the butter, onion and celery. Microwave at 90% power for 3 minutes, stirring halfway through the cooking.

2 Stir in the mushrooms then microwave at 90% power for 5 minutes.

3 Add the remaining ingredients; mix well. Cover, and microwave at 90% power for 4 to 5 minutes, or until heated through.

JAZZ IT UP!

Top this with Chinese noodles and, for fun, try using chopsticks. They're not that hard to use, and, while you're practicing, there'll be lots of laughs around the table!

Stuffed Turkey Breast Dinner

8 roll-ups

" Thanks to our microwaves, there's no reason to wait until Thanksgiving to enjoy turkey with all the fixin's. All we do is pop these roll-ups in the microwave and we're ready to celebrate…at any time of year! "

1 package (8 ounces)
    herb stuffing cubes
1/2 cup dried cranberries
1 can (14 ounces)
    ready-to-use chicken broth
8 turkey breast cutlets
    (about 2 pounds total)
2 jars (12 ounces each)
    turkey gravy

1 Coat a microwave-safe 9" x 13" baking dish with nonstick cooking spray. In a large bowl, combine the stuffing, dried cranberries, and broth; mix well.

2 Place the turkey cutlets on a work surface and place an equal amount of the stuffing mixture in the center of each. Roll up each cutlet and place seam side down in the baking dish.

3 Pour the gravy over the roll-ups. Cover, and microwave for 14 to 18 minutes at 70% power, or until heated through and no pink remains in the turkey.

GREAT GO-ALONG:

Since these are practically a complete meal by themselves, all you have to add is your favorite veggie and a big appetite!

Photo Page 107

Crunchy Turkey Bake

4 to 6 servings

" We always tend to have plenty of turkey to go around after a big roast turkey dinner. What can we make with it other than the usual sandwiches? Boy, have I got a leftover-lovin' idea for you! "

1 pound leftover cooked turkey,
    cut into 1/2-inch chunks
2 cans (15 ounces each)
    mixed vegetables, drained
1 can (10-3/4 ounces) condensed
    cream of mushroom soup
1 can (8 ounces) sliced
    water chestnuts, drained
1 cup (4 ounces) shredded
    sharp Cheddar cheese
3/4 cup mayonnaise
1 small onion, finely chopped
2 ribs celery, finely chopped
1 cup French-fried onions
    (from a 2.8-ounce can)

1 Coat a microwave-safe 2-quart casserole dish with nonstick cooking spray.

2 In a large bowl, combine all the ingredients except the French-fried onions; mix well and spoon into the casserole dish.

3 Microwave at 80% power for 10 minutes. Top with the French-fried onions. Microwave at 80% power for 5 minutes, or until bubbly and heated through.

DID YOU KNOW...

that the Inverter microwave makes leftovers taste as good as they did the first time? Add 3 to 4 tablespoons of water, juice, broth or other cooking liquid to the leftovers, and cover loosely with plastic wrap. Use the reheat feature and your dish will be ready and fresh-tasting before you know it! Stir once during cooking.

Barbecued Turkey Drumsticks
3 servings

“ I know what you're thinking, 'Barbecued drumsticks made in the microwave? It can't be done.' Well, believe it! The Inverter can give us tender, juicy drumsticks bursting with flavor – without firing up the grill! ”

3 turkey drumsticks
1/2 cup ketchup
2 tablespoons lemon juice
2 tablespoons butter, melted
2 tablespoons light brown sugar
1/2 of a small onion, finely chopped
1 garlic clove, minced
1 tablespoon yellow mustard
1 tablespoon Worcestershire sauce

1 Place the drumsticks in a microwave-safe 9" x 13" baking dish. In a medium bowl, combine the remaining ingredients; mix well and pour over the drumsticks.

2 Cover the dish with plastic wrap and microwave at 80% power for 20 minutes.

3 Carefully remove the plastic wrap and microwave for 5 more minutes. Serve with the sauce from the dish.

FINISHING TOUCH:

Serve these tangy turkey legs with creamy potato salad or coleslaw and hot corn bread for a picnic-perfect meal!

Roast Beef "Crepes"
8 crepes, 4 to 6 servings

" When we think of crepes, we usually think of dessert crepes filled with luscious berries and other sweet fillings. How about putting a whole new spin on the traditional style of crepes? Give it a try! "

2 cups warm prepared
    mashed potatoes
1 can (15 ounces) mixed
    vegetables, drained
8 thick slices deli-style
    roast beef (about 1-1/4 pounds)
1 jar (12 ounces) beef gravy
1/2 cup water

1 In a medium bowl, combine the mashed potatoes and mixed vegetables; mix well.

2 Place an equal amount of the mixture at one end of each roast beef slice; roll up crepe-style. Place seam side down in a microwave-safe 9" x 13" baking dish.

3 In a small bowl, combine the gravy and water; pour evenly over the "crepes."

4 Cover and microwave at 80% power for 6 to 8 minutes. Serve with the gravy spooned over the "crepes."

UNLIMITED OPTIONS:
For quick microwave mashed potatoes, combine the water, milk, butter, and salt in a microwave-safe bowl according to the package directions for instant mashed potato flakes. Stir in the potato flakes then use the potatoes as directed above.

Main Courses

All-in-One Goulash Bake

4 to 6 servings

" I love one-pot dishes! We get an all-in-one meal with easy preparation and cleanup which means no fuss and no mess! "

1 pound ground beef
1 jar (32 ounces) spaghetti sauce
1/2 cup water
1 green bell pepper, chopped
1 onion, chopped
2 garlic cloves, minced
1-1/2 cups cooked elbow macaroni
1-1/2 cups (6 ounces) shredded
    mozzarella cheese, divided
1/2 teaspoon salt
1/2 teaspoon black pepper

1 Crumble the beef into a microwave-safe 3-quart casserole dish. Microwave at 80% power for 3 to 4 minutes, or until no pink remains.

2 Stir in the spaghetti sauce, water, bell pepper, onion, garlic, macaroni, 1 cup mozzarella cheese, the salt, and pepper. Microwave at 80% power for 15 to 16 minutes, stirring halfway through the cooking.

3 Sprinkle the remaining 1/2 cup mozzarella cheese over the top of the goulash. Microwave at 80% power for 1 to 2 minutes, or until the cheese melts. Let stand for 5 minutes before serving.

DID YOU KNOW...

that many foods continue to cook (by conduction) even after their microwave cooking cycles are finished? For instance, by covering a casserole dish with foil and allowing it to stand after cooking for 5 to 10 minutes, the food will continue to cook in the center without overcooking its edges! That's what we call "stand time."

Mini Meat Loaves

4 servings

" Don't let these babies fool you. They may be smaller than the average meat loaf, but they're bigger on flavor! Try 'em tonight! "

1 pound ground beef
1/2 cup stuffing mix
1 small onion, chopped
1 egg
1 can (10-3/4 ounces)
    condensed tomato soup, divided
1/4 teaspoon salt

1 In a large bowl, combine the ground beef, stuffing mix, onion, egg, 1/2 cup soup, and the salt; mix well.

2 Shape the beef mixture into 4 mini loaves. Place the loaves in a microwave-safe 8-inch square baking dish. Pour the remaining soup over the loaves.

3 Microwave at 80% power for 10 minutes, or until no pink remains in the beef. Serve topped with the sauce from the baking dish.

UNLIMITED OPTIONS:

Served up with potatoes or rice and healthy greens, we've got a hearty meal ready in no time. Think it's impossible to make these any quicker? Make them in advance and freeze them. Take out as many as you need and use the Inverter's defrost feature to get a homemade dinner on the table in a snap!

Italian Meatballs

15 meatballs

" Who doesn't love a heaping bowl of spaghetti and meatballs? Why, it's quick, easy, and solves our dinnertime dilemma in a hurry. And nothing makes the pasta more perfect than hearty meatballs we make with our own two hands. "

1 pound ground beef
3/4 cup plain bread crumbs
1/2 cup water
1/4 cup coarsely chopped
    fresh parsley
1 egg
1-1/2 teaspoons garlic powder
1 teaspoon salt
1 teaspoon black pepper
1 jar (28 ounces) spaghetti sauce
1/3 cup grated Parmesan cheese
1 cup (4 ounces) shredded
    mozzarella cheese

FINISHING TOUCH: Make an Italian feast by serving these over warm spaghetti or on toasted hero rolls along with a crisp garden salad.

1 Coat a microwave-safe 9" x 13" baking dish with nonstick cooking spray.

2 In a large bowl, combine the ground beef, bread crumbs, water, parsley, egg, garlic powder, salt, and pepper; mix well. Form the mixture into 15 meatballs, and place in the baking dish.

3 In a medium bowl, combine the spaghetti sauce and Parmesan cheese; pour over the meatballs. Cover with plastic wrap and microwave at 70% power for 12 minutes, or until the meatballs are completely cooked through and the juices run clear.

4 Remove the plastic wrap and sprinkle the meatballs with the mozzarella cheese. Microwave at 70% power for 1 to 1-1/2 minutes, or until the cheese is melted.

Fiesta Tacos

8 tacos

❝ Make cooking fun for the whole family and get the kids involved by having a 'make your own tacos' dinner. With chips and salsa, and some lively Mexican music, you'll get everybody in the mood for a tasty good time! ❞

1/2 green bell pepper, chopped
1 pound ground beef
2 tablespoons taco seasoning
1/2 cup salsa
8 taco shells
1 cup (4 ounces) shredded
    Cheddar cheese
1 cup shredded lettuce
1 tomato, chopped

1 Place the green pepper in a 2-quart microwave-safe bowl and crumble the ground beef over it. Microwave at 80% power for 4 minutes, or until no pink remains in the beef; drain.

2 Stir in the taco seasoning and salsa; mix well. Cover and microwave at 70% power for 3 minutes.

3 Divide the meat mixture equally into the taco shells and top with cheese, lettuce, and tomato. Serve immediately.

UNLIMITED OPTIONS:

Serve these up at your next party as is or topped with guacamole and sour cream. Don't forget the refried beans and nachos as go-alongs.

M ain Courses

Fire Station Chili

4 servings

" Sound the alarm – there's a kitchen emergency! We need a quick-fix meal that'll satisfy everybody, even the pickiest of eaters! Don't worry – this recipe will save the day! "

1 tablespoon vegetable oil
1 small onion, chopped
2 garlic cloves, minced
1 pound ground beef
1 can (16 ounces) red
    kidney beans, drained
1 can (14 ounces) crushed tomatoes
3 tablespoons chili powder
1 tablespoon ground cumin
1 teaspoon salt
1/2 teaspoon black pepper

1 In a 3-quart microwave-safe casserole dish, combine the oil, onion, and garlic. Microwave at 90% power for 1-1/2 to 2 minutes, or until the onion is tender.

2 Crumble the ground beef into the onion mixture. Microwave at 80% power for 4 minutes, or until no pink remains in the meat; drain.

3 Add the remaining ingredients; mix well. Cover and microwave at 80% power for 8 minutes, stirring halfway through the cooking. Serve immediately.

DID YOU KNOW...

that you can use the Inverter microwave to easily cook ground beef? Simply place it in a microwave-safe bowl then, for 1 pound, cook on 100% power for 4 to 5 minutes. (For different amounts, adjust cooking time accordingly.) Place the cooked beef in a colander to drain well.

Homestyle Sloppy Joes
6 servings

" I can still remember making these messy-but-yummy sandwiches for my kids when they were growing up. Now they can make 'em even easier for their kids – and so can you! Of course, the sandwiches are still pretty messy, but that's the fun of eating 'em! "

1 pound ground beef
1 small onion, chopped
1/2 medium-sized green
    bell pepper, chopped
1 can (15 ounces) tomato sauce
1 tablespoon light brown sugar
1/4 teaspoon garlic powder
1/4 teaspoon salt
1/8 teaspoon black pepper
6 hamburger buns, split

1 In a 3-quart microwave-safe bowl, crumble the ground beef; stir in the onion and green pepper. Microwave at 80% power for 4 minutes, or until no pink remains in the beef, stirring halfway through the cooking; drain.

2 Add the tomato sauce, brown sugar, garlic powder, salt, and black pepper; mix well. Microwave at 80% power for 6 minutes, stirring halfway through the cooking time.

3 Spoon onto the split buns and serve.

DID YOU KNOW...

that the microwave can help us peel onions? Yup, it sure can! Simply place an onion in a microwave-safe bowl and heat for 30 to 45 seconds. Squeeze the onion at the root end until it pops out of its peel.

Curried Lamb

4 to 6 servings

" If you've always turned up your nose at lamb, this recipe might just change how you feel about it. By teaming lamb with spices like ginger and curry, we've got an international specialty that'll knock your socks off! "

1 tablespoon butter
2 medium onions, chopped
3 garlic cloves, minced
2 tablespoons all-purpose flour
1/4 teaspoon ground ginger
2 tablespoons curry powder
1/4 teaspoon ground red pepper
1-1/4 teaspoons salt
2 pounds boneless leg of lamb
    or lamb stew meat,
      cut into 1-inch chunks
1 can (15 ounces) coconut milk
1 package (9 ounces) frozen cut
    green beans, thawed
1/2 cup raisins

1 In a large microwave-safe bowl, combine the butter, onions, and garlic. Microwave at 90% power for 3 minutes, or until the onion is tender.

2 In another large bowl, combine the flour, ginger, curry, red pepper, and salt; mix well. Add the lamb chunks; toss to coat well then add to the onion mixture.

3 Microwave at 100% power for 4 minutes; stir then microwave for 4 more minutes, or until no pink remains in the lamb.

4 Add the coconut milk, green beans, and raisins. Microwave at 80% power for 12 to 14 minutes, or until the lamb is tender.

DID YOU KNOW...

what to look for when buying lamb? It should have a fine-grained flesh and creamy, white fat. Also, the plumper the better!

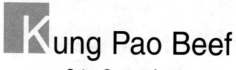

Kung Pao Beef

6 to 8 servings

" Break out the chopsticks for this traditional Chinese dish that gives you the taste of the Orient in minutes! "

1/2 cup teriyaki sauce
2 tablespoons cornstarch
1 teaspoon crushed red pepper
1/2 teaspoon ground ginger
One 2-pound flank steak, thinly sliced
2/3 cup salted peanuts
4 scallions, thinly sliced

1 Coat a microwave-safe 9" x 13" baking dish with nonstick cooking spray.

2 Add the teriyaki sauce, cornstarch, crushed red pepper, and ginger to the baking dish; mix well. Add the flank steak and turn to coat completely with the sauce.

3 Microwave at 90% power for 6 minutes, stirring halfway through the cooking time.

4 Sprinkle with the peanuts and scallions, and serve.

FINISHING TOUCH:

Serve this Asian specialty over a bed of warm rice or maybe even some Chinese rice noodles for a flavor-packed change-of-pace main course.

Photo at right

Kung Pao Beef
Ready in less than 10 Minutes

Roasted Acorn Squash
Ready in less than 30 Minutes

Autumn Sweet Potatoes
Ready in less than 10 Minutes

Stuffed Turkey Breast Dinner
Ready in less than 20 Minutes

Herb-Crusted Pork Tenderloin
Ready in less than 15 Minutes

Herb-Crusted Pork Tenderloin

4 to 6 servings

" This is one dish you won't wanna miss out on! Using a rub for the pork seals in extra flavor and juices. It's a cooking preparation that we can use on almost any type of meat. "

2 pork tenderloins
   (about 2 pounds total)
2 tablespoons water
1 teaspoon browning
   and seasoning sauce
1 tablespoon chopped fresh parsley
1 teaspoon garlic powder
1/2 teaspoon rubbed sage
1/2 teaspoon salt
1/2 teaspoon black pepper

1 Place the pork in a microwave-safe 7" x 11" baking dish. In a small bowl, combine the water and the browning and seasoning sauce; mix well then spoon over the pork.

2 In another small bowl, combine the remaining ingredients; mix well then rub evenly over the pork.

3 Cover the baking dish and microwave the pork at 70% power for 6 minutes. Let the pork stand in the microwave for 3 minutes. Slice and serve with the pan drippings.

UNLIMITED OPTIONS:

We can brown our meat in a variety of ways so, besides using browning and seasoning sauce, try soy or barbecue sauce, marmalade, or even brown gravy. Mmm!

Photo at left

Sweet-and-Sour Pork

4 to 6 servings

❝ It'll take more time to order this dish and wait for the Chinese restaurant to deliver it than it will to make it yourself! So what are you waiting for?! **❞**

2 pounds boneless pork sirloin,
  cut into bite-sized pieces
1 tablespoon oil
1 tablespoon cornstarch
2 bell peppers (1 red, 1 green),
  cut into thin strips
1/4 teaspoon ground red pepper
1/2 teaspoon salt
1 can (8 ounces) pineapple
  chunks, drained
1-1/2 cups sweet-and-sour sauce

1 Place the pork in a microwave-safe 9" x 13" baking dish. Drizzle with the oil and sprinkle with the cornstarch. Place the pepper strips over the pork; cover, and microwave at 100% power for 5 minutes.

2 Season the pork with the ground red pepper and salt. Toss the pineapple chunks with the sweet-and-sour sauce; pour over the pork, cover, and microwave at 80% power for 6 minutes, stirring halfway through the cooking time.

GREAT GO-ALONG:

Make it a complete meal by serving this tangy, juicy pork dish over a bed of cooked rice.

Complete Pork Chop Dinner
6 servings

" Say goodbye to plain old pork chops 'cause this recipe's gonna have the whole family running to the table! "

2/3 cup instant rice
1 can (14-1/2 ounces) stewed tomatoes
1 can (16 ounces) kidney beans,
    rinsed and drained
1 can (15-1/4 ounces) whole-kernel
    corn, drained
6 pork loin chops,
    1/2 inch thick (2 pounds total)
1 tablespoon vegetable oil
1/2 teaspoon salt
1/2 teaspoon black pepper
1/2 cup salsa
1 teaspoon chili powder

1 Coat a microwave-safe 9" x 13" baking dish with nonstick cooking spray. Sprinkle the rice over the bottom of the dish. Spread the stewed tomatoes evenly over the rice.

2 In a medium bowl, combine the kidney beans and corn; mix well and reserve 1/2 cup of the mixture. Sprinkle the remaining corn mixture over the stewed tomatoes.

3 Brush the pork chops with the oil and season with the salt and pepper. Place in the baking dish over the corn mixture.

4 In a small bowl, combine the salsa and chili powder; spread evenly over the pork chops. Sprinkle with the reserved corn mixture.

5 Cover the baking dish with plastic wrap and microwave at 80% power for 12 minutes, or until the rice is tender and the pork chops are cooked through.

Ham and Scalloped Potato Casserole
6 to 8 servings

" Here's the perfect go-along for breakfast or dinner. And if there's any left over, it's just the thing to pop in the microwave to reheat and get you over the 'Gee, I'm hungry' hump. "

3/4 pound deli ham, sliced
   1/2-inch thick and
   cut into 1/2-inch chunks
1 package (16 ounces) frozen
   shredded hash brown potatoes
1 package (10 ounces) frozen peas
2 cans (10-3/4 ounces each)
   condensed cream of celery soup
1-1/2 cups milk
1 teaspoon onion powder
1/2 teaspoon salt
1 teaspoon black pepper
1-1/2 cups coarsely crushed
   butter-flavored crackers

1 In a large bowl, combine all the ingredients except the crackers; mix well.

2 Pour the mixture into a microwave-safe 9" x 13" baking dish and sprinkle with the crushed crackers.

3 Microwave at 90% power for 20 minutes, or until heated through.

DID YOU KNOW...

that there's a secret to freezing casseroles so they'll taste great after reheating? Cook the casserole then, before wrapping, place a paper cup in the center of the dish. When it's time to thaw the casserole in the microwave, leave the cup in place, add 3 to 4 tablespoons of water to the cup, cover loosely with plastic wrap, and use the reheat function.

Ham with Raisin Sauce
2 to 3 servings

" This holiday favorite doesn't have to be kept aside until a celebration. Uh uh! Make any night a special occasion, without any of that dreaded holiday stress! "

One 1-pound ham steak
1/2 cup apple juice
2 tablespoons packed
    light brown sugar
1-1/2 teaspoons cornstarch
1/2 teaspoon dry mustard
1/4 cup raisins

1 Coat a microwave-safe 9" x 13" baking dish with nonstick cooking spray. Place the ham in the dish.

2 Combine the remaining ingredients; mix well and spoon over the ham.

3 Cover, and microwave at 80% power for 5 to 6 minutes, or until the sauce thickens and the ham is heated through.

FINISHING TOUCH:

It's easy to give this a holiday-fancy look by surrounding the ham with sliced red and green apples, and more raisins just before serving.

Lemon Dill Salmon

3 to 4 servings

" Looking for a fresh catch? Reel in a true winner with this light and flaky fish that's bound to have your dinner guests showing up early every time! "

One 1-pound salmon fillet
1/4 teaspoon salt
1/4 teaspoon black pepper
1 lemon, thinly sliced
1 bunch fresh dill
1 tablespoon olive oil

1 Coat a microwave-safe 7" x 11" baking dish with nonstick cooking spray.

2 Place the salmon fillet skin side down in the dish; season with the salt and pepper.

3 Place lemon slices and sprigs of dill in alternating rows across the top of the fish. Drizzle with the oil.

4 Microwave at 80% power for 5 minutes, or until the fish flakes easily with a fork.

Red Snapper with Lime Sauce

4 servings

" After your gang sinks their teeth into this luscious, lime-infused snapper, they'll flip when you tell them how simple it was! "

4 red snapper fillets
   (about 1-1/2 pounds total)
1/8 teaspoon salt
1/8 teaspoon black pepper
1 lime
1/4 cup (1/2 stick) butter,
   cut into thin slices
1 tablespoon chopped fresh parsley
1 lime, cut into wedges (optional)

1 Place the snapper fillets in a microwave-safe 9" x 13" baking dish; season with the salt and pepper. Squeeze the lime over the fish, and top with the butter slices.

2 Cover the baking dish, and microwave at 80% power for 4 minutes.

3 Uncover the dish and sprinkle the fillets with parsley; microwave uncovered for 3 to 4 more minutes, or until the fish flakes easily with a fork. Garnish with lime wedges, if desired.

UNLIMITED OPTIONS:

Can't find red snapper? Just pick up your favorite white-fleshed fish fillets and cook 'em up this way.

Trout Amandine

3 to 4 servings

" Our Inverter microwave lets us turn any night into an extraordinary event. It keeps giving us more and more interesting, quick dinner options like this delicate dish. "

1 pound trout fillets
1/4 teaspoon salt
1/4 teaspoon paprika
2 tablespoons butter,
    cut into small pieces
1/4 cup sliced almonds
1 tablespoon chopped fresh parsley

1 Coat a microwave-safe 7" x 11" baking dish with nonstick cooking spray.

2 Place the trout fillets in the baking dish; season with the salt and paprika. Place the butter on the fish then sprinkle with the almonds and parsley.

3 Microwave at 80% power for 4 to 5 minutes, or until the fish flakes easily with a fork.

DID YOU KNOW...

that we can easily defrost frozen fish fillets in the Inverter microwave? Rinse the frozen fillets with cold water and allow them to stand for 5 minutes. Place the fillets in a microwave-safe dish and microwave for 4 to 6 minutes per pound on Power Level 3, turning the fillets over once during the cycle.

Saucy Lemon–Pepper Shrimp

4 to 6 servings

" The next time company is due, impress them with this elegant dinner. It looks fancy-schmancy, but takes only minutes to prepare. And with this all-in-one dish, cleanup is just as easy, so you'll have time to visit with your guests. "

1-1/2 pounds uncooked large
   shrimp, peeled and
   deveined, with tails left on
1/2 teaspoon salt
1 teaspoon black pepper
1/2 cup (1 stick) butter,
   thinly sliced
Juice and zest of 2 lemons
1 tablespoon chopped fresh parsley

1 Place the shrimp in a microwave-safe 9" x 13" baking dish; season with the salt and pepper then top with the butter, lemon zest, and parsley; pour the lemon juice into the baking dish.

2 Microwave at 80% power for 4 to 4-1/2 minutes, or until the shrimp are pink and cooked through, stirring halfway through the cooking.

GREAT GO-ALONG:

Spoon the shrimp over a bed of steaming cooked rice or pasta to make sure you don't miss any of this rich, lemony sauce!

Photo Page 2

Shrimp Diavolo

4 servings

" Why is this called 'diavolo'? Because it's devilishly spicy! Go ahead – enjoy it. After all, there's a little devil in all of us! **"**

1 can (14-1/2 ounces) diced tomatoes
2 garlic cloves, minced
1 teaspoon dried basil
1 teaspoon dried oregano
1/2 teaspoon crushed red pepper
1/2 teaspoon sugar
1 teaspoon salt
1 pound uncooked large
    shrimp, peeled and
    deveined, with tails left on

1 In a microwave-safe 9" x 13" baking dish, combine all the ingredients except the shrimp; mix well then stir in the shrimp.

2 Microwave at 80% power for 5 to 6 minutes, or until the shrimp are no longer pink, stirring halfway through the cooking.

Quick Shrimp Gumbo

4 servings

" Bring home the tastes and flavors of New Orleans with this jazzed-up quick gumbo. The spicy kick of the salsa and tomatoes make it seem like our taste buds are having a festival! "

1/2 pound large cooked
    shrimp, peeled and deveined
1 cup salsa
1 package (16 ounces)
    frozen cut okra,
    thawed and drained
1 can (14-1/2 ounces) stewed
    Mexican-style tomatoes
2 cups warm cooked rice

1 Combine all the ingredients except the rice in a large microwave-safe bowl.

2 Cover, and microwave at 80% power for 7 to 8 minutes, or until thick and heated through; stir.

3 Serve in individual bowls mixed with rice.

DID YOU KNOW...

that gumbo is a Creole specialty that's a staple of New Orleans cuisine and continues to grow in popularity around the world? The best part about gumbo is that we can add or substitute chicken, sausage, and other shellfish to give it variety every time we make it.

Chunky Veggie Chili
6 to 8 servings

" When you want a hot and hearty bowl of meatless chili, look no further! This recipe is full of so much down-home flavor, you won't even miss the meat! "

1 tablespoon olive oil
1 large onion, chopped
1 large red bell pepper, chopped
1 large zucchini, chopped
1 medium-sized yellow
    squash, chopped
2 cans (14-1/2 ounces each)
    diced tomatoes, undrained
2/3 cup salsa
1-1/2 teaspoons ground cumin
1-1/2 teaspoons chili powder
2 cans (16 ounces each) red
    kidney beans, rinsed and drained

1 In a large microwave-safe bowl, combine the oil and onion. Microwave at 90% power for 2 minutes, or until the onion is tender.

2 Add the red pepper, zucchini, and yellow squash; mix well and cover with plastic wrap. Microwave at 90% power for 5 minutes, or until the vegetables are tender.

3 Stir in the diced tomatoes, salsa, cumin, and chili powder. Cover, and microwave at 90% power for 12 to 15 minutes. Stir in the kidney beans and microwave at 90% power for 1 to 2 minutes, or until heated through.

UNLIMITED
OPTIONS:

If you have leftovers, not to worry! This chili tastes great on the second day too! Just reheat in your Inverter microwave, and enjoy!

Main Courses

Garden-Fresh Burgers

6 servings

❝ If you've never had a really good veggie burger, you're missing out! Not only are they good for you, they're really full-flavored, and just as filling as traditional ground-beef burgers! ❞

3/4 cup plain bread crumbs, divided
3 cups warm cooked brown rice
1 medium carrot, peeled and grated
1/2 small onion, grated
1/3 cup chopped fresh parsley
1/4 cup grated Parmesan cheese
2 garlic cloves, minced
3 tablespoons soy sauce
2 eggs, beaten
1 teaspoon dried thyme
1 tablespoon vegetable oil
3 tablespoons duck sauce

UNLIMITED OPTIONS:

Instant brown rice is a great option for this. Just prepare it using the microwave directions on the package.

1 Coat a microwave-safe 9" x 13" baking dish with nonstick cooking spray. Place 1/2 cup bread crumbs in a shallow dish; set aside.

2 In a large bowl, combine the rice, carrot, onion, parsley, Parmesan cheese, garlic, soy sauce, eggs, thyme, and remaining 1/4 cup bread crumbs; mix well. Form the mixture into 6 equal-sized patties. Coat the patties with the reserved bread crumbs and place in the baking dish.

3 Brush each patty with vegetable oil. Microwave at 80% power for 6 minutes, or until set and heated through. Top each burger with duck sauce and serve.

Black Bean Enchiladas
4 to 5 servings

" What's faster – going out to a local Mexican restaurant or creating those tastes and smells right in your own kitchen? Why go out when you can make these ooey gooey enchiladas in a flash – and without paying restaurant prices?! "

1 tablespoon vegetable oil
1 medium onion, chopped
3 garlic cloves, minced
2 cans (15 ounces each)
    black beans, drained
1 can (15-1/4 ounces) whole-kernel
    corn, drained
Ten 8-inch flour tortillas
2 cups Mexican cheese
    blend, divided
1 jar (16 ounces) salsa

1 Coat a microwave-safe 9" x 13" baking dish with nonstick cooking spray.

2 In a medium-sized microwave-safe bowl, combine the oil, onion, and garlic. Microwave at 80% power for 3 minutes, or until the onion is tender. Add the beans and corn; mix well.

3 Divide the bean mixture equally down the center of each tortilla, sprinkle each with 2 table-spoons cheese, and roll up tightly. Place the tortillas seam side down in the baking dish. Spread the salsa over the tortillas.

4 Cover, and microwave at 80% power for 6 minutes. Sprinkle the remaining cheese over the top of the tortillas. Microwave at 80% power for 1 minute, or until heated through and the cheese is melted.

DID YOU KNOW...

it's easy to keep your microwave smelling fresh? Simply combine 1 to 1-1/2 cups of water with the juice and peel of one lemon in a microwave-safe bowl. Microwave at 100% power for 5 minutes then remove the bowl and wipe down the interior of the oven with a damp cloth.

Side Dishes

Asparagus with Hollandaise Sauce

2 to 4 servings

" Sometimes the simplest things are the best. And what better than fancy asparagus drizzled with homemade hollandaise sauce to prove that? "

1 pound fresh asparagus,
    trimmed
1/4 cup water
1/2 teaspoon plus 1/8 teaspoon
    salt, divided
1/4 cup (1/2 stick) butter
2 egg yolks
2 teaspoons fresh lemon juice

1 Place the asparagus (tips toward center) in a microwave-safe 7" x 11" baking dish. Add the water and season with 1/2 teaspoon salt. Cover and microwave at 90% power for 5 minutes; remove and set aside.

2 In a small microwave-safe bowl, heat the butter at 90% power for 40 seconds, until melted. In a small bowl, beat the egg yolks, lemon juice, and remaining 1/8 teaspoon salt until thick. Slowly pour in the melted butter, whisking well. Microwave uncovered at 40% power for 30 seconds, stirring halfway through the cooking time.

3 Uncover the asparagus; drain, and place on a serving platter. Drizzle with the hollandaise sauce and serve immediately.

DID YOU KNOW...

that we can freshen up wilted asparagus tips by soaking them in cold water before cooking? This can be a real help when you want to make a big impression!

Photo Page 108

Glazed Baby Carrots

4 to 6 servings

" No more ho-hum carrots on our dinner plates! Uh uh! These are so sweet and tangy, even the kids will love 'em! "

1 pound baby carrots
2 tablespoons water
1/2 cup packed brown sugar
2 tablespoons butter
2 tablespoons white vinegar
1/4 teaspoon cornstarch

1 In a medium-sized microwave-safe bowl, combine the carrots and water; cover and microwave at 90% power for 5 to 6 minutes, or until crisp-tender. Uncover and drain.

2 In another medium-sized microwave-safe bowl, combine the remaining ingredients. Microwave at 80% power for 1 to 1-1/2 minutes, or until the mixture is melted and thickened.

3 Pour the glaze over the carrots, mix until well coated, and serve.

Photo Page 107

Side Dishes

erbed Broccoli

4 servings

" Broccoli is really versatile, and it goes with just about anything from meat and fish to pasta and poultry. As a matter of fact, made this way, it's so good that you might just want to eat it all by itself! "

2 tablespoons olive oil
1 teaspoon lemon juice
1 garlic clove, minced
1/4 teaspoon dried oregano
1/4 teaspoon dried basil
1/2 teaspoon salt
1/4 teaspoon black pepper
2 packages (10 ounces each)
    frozen broccoli florets,
    thawed and drained

1 In a microwave-safe 9" x 13" baking dish, combine all the ingredients except the broccoli; mix well. Add the broccoli and toss until well coated.

2 Cover and microwave at 80% power for 4 minutes, or until heated through. Serve immediately.

HEALTHIER OPTION:

A member of the cabbage family, broccoli is a great source of Vitamins A and C, and is low in fat and sodium... so dig in!

Cauliflower and Broccoli Bake

8 to 10 servings

" If you ever thought broccoli and cauliflower were boring, think again! The combination of creamy and crispy makes this a go-along that'll turn you into a dinnertime hero! **"**

1 package (16 ounces) frozen broccoli
1 package (16 ounces) frozen cauliflower
2 tablespoons water
1 can (14-3/4 ounces) cream-style corn
1 can (10-1/2 ounces) condensed
    cream of celery soup
1 can (2.8 ounces) French-fried
    onions, with 1/2 cup reserved
1-1/2 cups shredded sharp
    Cheddar cheese, divided
2 tablespoons finely chopped onion
1 teaspoon dried thyme

UNLIMITED OPTIONS:

Sure, you can use fresh broccoli and cauliflower for this dish, but don't be afraid to buy frozen. Inexpensive and ready to use, frozen veggies are a great way to save time and money!

1 Combine the broccoli, cauliflower, and water in a microwave-safe 9" x 13" baking dish. Cover and microwave at 90% power for 5 minutes. Stir, then microwave for 2 more minutes.

2 In a medium bowl, combine the corn, soup, French-fried onions, 1 cup cheese, the onion, and thyme; mix well then spoon over the vegetables. Microwave uncovered at 80% power for 5 minutes.

3 Top the mixture with the remaining 1/2 cup cheese and reserved French-fried onions. Microwave at 70% power for 2 minutes, or until the cheese is melted.

Side Dishes

Quick Roasted Peppers

6 to 8 servings

" Roasting peppers may sound like a lot of work, but we can have that traditional fire-roasted taste without heating up our kitchens, thanks to our Inverter microwaves! **"**

3 tablespoons vegetable oil
1/2 teaspoon garlic powder
3/4 teaspoon salt
1/4 teaspoon black pepper
4 bell peppers (red, green,
    or yellow), cut into strips

1 In a large bowl, combine the oil, garlic powder, salt, and pepper; mix well. Add the pepper strips and toss to coat completely; pour into a microwave-safe 9" x 13" baking dish.

2 Microwave at 90% power for 10 minutes then serve immediately.

DID YOU KNOW...

that bell peppers not only look and taste great, but they make handy serving bowls? Simply slice off the top inch of a pepper and scoop out the core and seeds to make it ready for holding a creamy dip or spread. Why not do a bunch in different colors?

Summer Veggie Medley
6 servings

" We all need our five-a-day servings of fruit and veggies, and sometimes we just have to spice things up. So here's a way to add a little summer sun and color to traditional veggies and make any day brighter! "

3 medium tomatoes,
    cut into small chunks
3 medium yellow squash,
    cut into 1/2-inch chunks
2 medium zucchini,
    cut into 1/2-inch chunks
3 garlic cloves, minced
2 tablespoons chopped fresh basil
2 tablespoons olive oil
2 teaspoons sugar
1 teaspoon dried thyme
1-1/2 teaspoons salt
1/2 teaspoon black pepper

1 In a large bowl, combine all the ingredients; toss until the vegetables are well coated then pour into a microwave-safe 9" x 13" baking dish.

2 Cover and microwave at 90% power for 15 minutes, stirring halfway through the cooking time.

Tropical Squash

4 servings

" Fast as can be, this go-along will practically transport you to the tropics. And it's so sweet, you won't believe it's not a dessert! "

1 package (12 ounces) frozen
   butternut squash, thawed
1/2 cup crushed pineapple, drained
1/4 cup packed light brown sugar
1/2 teaspoon ground cinnamon
2 egg whites, beaten

1 Coat a microwave-safe 1-quart casserole dish with nonstick cooking spray. Combine all the ingredients in a large bowl; mix well then pour into the casserole dish.

2 Microwave at 80% power for 10 to 12 minutes, or until the center is set. Serve immediately.

DID YOU KNOW...

that the Inverter microwave can help soften brown sugar? Simply place the sugar in a microwave-safe bowl and add a slice of white bread or a slice of fresh apple. Cover, and microwave on full power for 30 to 40 seconds. Let stand for 30 seconds, remove bread or apple, and stir!

Southern Corn Pudding

6 to 8 servings

" When we're in the mood for comfort food, what could be more satisfying than Southern-inspired dishes? And thanks to the speed of today's Inverter microwaves, we can have foods like this rich and creamy pudding in minutes! "

1 package (8-1/2 ounces)
    corn muffin mix
1 can (15-1/4 ounces)
    whole-kernel corn, drained
1 can (14-3/4 ounces)
    cream-style corn
1 cup sour cream
1/2 cup (1 stick) butter, softened
1 egg
1 tablespoon sugar
1/2 teaspoon salt

1 Coat a microwave-safe 2-quart casserole dish with nonstick cooking spray.

2 In a large bowl, combine all the ingredients; pour into the casserole dish.

3 Microwave at 70% power for 17 to 18 minutes, or until set. Let cool for 5 minutes before serving.

JAZZ IT UP!

If you'd like to give this a Southwestern flavor, add some shredded Monterey Jack cheese to the mix and garnish with chopped fresh chives after cooking.

Cheddar Carrot Pudding
6 to 9 servings

" Don't worry – we're not suggesting you add cheese and veggies to your favorite sweet dessert pudding! This is a rich, buttery side dish that's sure to please, 'cause it simply melts in your mouth. "

1 pound peeled fresh or frozen
    carrots, cooked and mashed
6 tablespoons butter, softened (see below)
4 eggs
1 cup cracker meal
3/4 cup (3 ounces) shredded
    Cheddar cheese
3/4 cup milk
1 tablespoon sugar
1-1/2 teaspoons dried dill weed
1 teaspoon onion powder
1 teaspoon salt

1 Coat a microwave-safe 8-inch square baking dish with nonstick cooking spray.

2 Place the mashed carrots in a large bowl; add the butter and mix well. Add the eggs one at a time, beating after each addition.

3 Stir in the remaining ingredients; pour into the baking dish and microwave at 80% power for 10 to 12 minutes, or until the center is set.

4 Cut into squares and serve.

DID YOU KNOW...

that we can soften butter in the Inverter microwave in just seconds? Simply unwrap 1 stick (1/4 pound) of butter and place it in a microwave-safe bowl. Microwave at 30% power for 10-second intervals until it reaches the desired consistency – and that's it! And another tip: 1 stick of butter is equal to 8 tablespoons.

Roasted Acorn Squash

4 to 6 servings

" Don't wait until the leaves start changing to enjoy this harvest-time treat! No matter what time of year it is, we can bring home the feel of autumn with this hearty side dish. "

2 medium acorn squash
1/3 cup vegetable oil
1/2 teaspoon salt
1/4 teaspoon black pepper

1 Pierce the squash a few times with a knife then place the whole squash in a microwave-safe 9" x 13" baking dish. Microwave at 80% power for 9 minutes.

2 Remove the squash from the microwave and let cool for 2 to 3 minutes. Cut in half and remove the seeds; cut squash into 2-inch chunks.

3 In a large bowl, combine the oil, salt, and pepper; mix well. Add the squash and toss until well coated then return the pieces to the baking dish.

4 Microwave at 80% power for 15 minutes, or until fork-tender; serve immediately.

FINISHING TOUCH:

Serve this as is to enjoy the delicate, nutty flavor of the squash, or drizzle it with warm maple syrup or melted butter and a sprinkle of cinnamon-sugar just before serving.

Photo Page 106

Side Dishes

Herbed Potato Wedges

4 servings

" These are so brown and tender, you won't believe they were made in a microwave! The secret is in the advanced Panasonic technology. "

2 tablespoons butter
1/4 teaspoon browning and
    seasoning sauce
1/2 teaspoon garlic powder
1/4 teaspoon dried basil
1/4 teaspoon salt
1/8 teaspoon black pepper
3 large potatoes, washed and
    cut into wedges

1 In a microwave-safe 7" x 11" baking dish, combine all the ingredients except the potatoes. Microwave at 90% power for 20 to 30 seconds, or until the butter is melted.

2 Add the potato wedges; toss to coat completely, and arrange the wedges in the baking dish in a single layer. Microwave at 90% power for 9 to 11 minutes, or until the potatoes are tender, stirring halfway through the cooking time.

UNLIMITED OPTIONS:

Serve these all by themselves or with your favorite dipping sauce – ketchup, barbecue sauce, ranch dressing, honey mustard, whatever you fancy!

Easy Potatoes au Gratin

6 to 8 servings

" The great thing about potatoes is that there's so much we can do with 'em! One of my favorite ways is cheesy au gratin-style and, after you try this version, I bet it'll be one of your favorites too! "

1 package (28 ounces)
   frozen O'Brien-style potatoes
   (with peppers and onions)
2 cans (10-3/4 ounces each)
   condensed cream of potato soup
1 cup sour cream
1 cup (4 ounces) shredded
   Cheddar cheese, divided
1/2 teaspoon salt
1/4 teaspoon black pepper

1 In a large bowl, combine the potatoes, soup, sour cream, 1/2 cup cheese, the salt, and pepper; mix well. Spoon into a microwave-safe 9" x 13" baking dish. Microwave at 90% power for 19 to 20 minutes.

2 Sprinkle with the remaining 1/2 cup cheese and microwave at 90% power for 2 minutes, or until the cheese is melted. Let stand for 5 minutes before serving.

FINISHING TOUCH:

Top the cooked potatoes with chopped scallions and bacon bits as a colorful garnish! And that's just the beginning! Add any of your other favorite toppings.

Smothered Potatoes

6 to 8 servings

" This homestyle go-along sure pairs well with our favorite cuts of meat. And talk about fast…you won't believe you can 'bake' up such old-fashioned flavor so quickly! "

4 to 5 medium potatoes, peeled
    and cut into 1/8-inch slices
1 small onion, thinly sliced
1/2 red bell pepper, chopped
3/4 teaspoon salt
1/2 teaspoon black pepper
1/4 cup (1/2 stick) butter, melted

1 Coat a microwave-safe 9" x 13" baking dish with nonstick cooking spray.

2 In a large bowl, combine all the ingredients; toss until the vegetables are well coated then pour into the baking dish.

3 Microwave at 80% power for 12 to 13 minutes, or until the potatoes are tender; mix gently. Serve immediately.

DID YOU KNOW...

this is a great dish to prepare in advance? Just slice the potatoes then dip them in a mixture of 1 quart cool water and 3 tablespoons lemon juice. Drain, cover, and refrigerate until you're ready to put the dish together and bake it. Why dip the potatoes? 'Cause their flesh will begin to darken once it's exposed to air.

Spiral Baked Potatoes

4 servings

"" Okay, if you're tired of the same old side dishes night after night, and are ready for something new and exciting, here's the answer that'll turn your gang into fans for life! ""

4 medium potatoes, washed
4 tablespoons (1/2 stick) butter
1 tablespoon fresh lemon juice
   (see Note)
1/4 cup grated Parmesan cheese
3 tablespoons chopped fresh parsley
2 teaspoons grated lemon peel
   (optional)

DID YOU KNOW…

that when you need just a few drops of fresh lemon juice there's an easy way to do it? Simply pierce the skin of a lemon with a toothpick and squeeze out what you need. When you're finished, insert the toothpick back into the hole, place the lemon in a plastic bag, and keep refrigerated until needed again.

1 Place 2 wooden spoons parallel to one another on a work surface and place a potato lengthwise between the handles. Make at least 8 crosswise slits three-quarters of the way through the potato, stopping each time the knife hits the spoon handles. Repeat with the remaining potatoes, and place them in a microwave-safe 7" x 11" baking dish.

2 In a small bowl, combine the butter and lemon juice. Microwave at 90% power for 40 to 50 seconds, or until the butter is melted. Brush the butter mixture over the potatoes and between the slices. Microwave at 100% power for 6 minutes.

3 Brush the potatoes again with any butter mixture from the bottom of the baking dish. Microwave at 100% power for 4 to 5 minutes, or until tender. (NOTE: Cooking time will vary depending on the size of your potatoes.)

4 In a small bowl, combine the remaining ingredients; mix well and sprinkle over the potatoes and between the slices. Cover with plastic wrap and let stand for 5 minutes before serving.

 **Side Dishes**

Cheesy Stuffed Potatoes

4 servings

" It's amazing – with seven everyday ingredients and our Inverter microwave, we can serve up fancy stuffed spuds without heating up the kitchen! "

4 large potatoes, washed
4 tablespoons (1/2 stick) butter
4 ounces cream cheese
2 scallions, thinly sliced
1/4 cup milk
1/4 teaspoon salt
1/4 teaspoon black pepper

1 Using a fork, pierce the potatoes several times. Microwave at 90% power for 12 to 14 minutes, or until tender. Cut a 1/4-inch slice lengthwise off the top of each potato; carefully scoop out the pulp, leaving the shells intact.

2 In a medium-sized microwave-safe bowl, combine the butter and cream cheese. Microwave at 90% power for 30 to 40 seconds, or until the cream cheese is softened. Add the potato pulp, scallions, milk, salt, and pepper; mix well. Stuff the potato shells with the mixture, and place on a microwave-safe dish.

3 Microwave at 90% power for 2 to 2-1/2 minutes, or until heated through.

HEALTHIER OPTION:

Potato skin contains loads of flavor and good-for-you nutrients, so be sure to enjoy every last bite!

Autumn Sweet Potatoes

6 to 8 servings

" This dish shouts 'autumn!' and 'sweet flavor!' so, since all the ingredients are available year-round, you can make it any time you want the gang to shout 'Hurray for you!' "

1 can (40 ounces) sweet potatoes
    or yams, drained and
    cut into chunks
1 can (8 ounces) pineapple
    chunks, drained
1 can (16 ounces) sliced
    carrots, drained
1/4 cup packed light brown sugar
1 cup mini marshmallows

1 Place the sweet potatoes in a microwave-safe 7" x 11" baking dish. Top with the pineapple and carrots then sprinkle with the brown sugar. Microwave at 70% power for 4 minutes.

2 Sprinkle with the marshmallows then microwave at 70% power for 3 minutes, or until the marshmallows are melted.

FINISHING TOUCH:

Just before serving, sprinkle the top with ground cinnamon or nutmeg, or even some grated orange zest for extra rich flavor and freshness.

Photo Page 106

 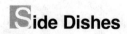

Quick Popcorn Stuffing
6 to 8 servings

" And you thought the microwave was only handy for popping up snacks! Well, it does work well for that, but wait 'til you use your Inverter model for cooking up this popcorn stuffing! You'll be a microwave convert, just like me! **"**

6 cups crumbled corn bread
    or corn muffins
4 cups popped popcorn (see Tip)
1 medium onion, finely chopped
1 cup chicken broth
1/4 cup (1/2 stick) butter, melted
2 eggs
1-1/2 teaspoons rubbed sage

1 Coat a microwave-safe 8-inch square baking dish with nonstick cooking spray.

2 In a large bowl, combine all the ingredients; mix well then spoon into the baking dish.

3 Microwave at 80% power for 8 minutes, or until the center is set. Cut into squares and serve.

PREPARATION TIP:

One regular package of microwave popcorn yields 7 to 8 cups of popcorn. And you don't have to throw away the unused popcorn. Save what doesn't go into the dressing, drizzle it with melted butter, and enjoy it with a movie after dinner.

Easy Dumplings

12 dumplings

"Who can resist fresh dumplings? These are light, fluffy, and a nice change-of-pace go-along."

3 cups self-rising flour
1-1/2 cups milk
1/3 cup mayonnaise
2 tablespoons butter, melted
1/8 teaspoon paprika

1 In a medium bowl, combine the flour, milk, and mayonnaise; mix well. Spoon evenly into a microwave-safe 12-cup muffin pan.

2 In a small bowl, combine the butter and paprika; mix well then brush over the dumpling batter.

3 Microwave at 70% power for 8 minutes, or until cooked through.

Old-Fashioned Baked Beans
6 to 8 servings

" You might think that these homestyle beans can't be made in the microwave but, thanks to Inverter technology, in minutes we can have the same homestyle taste and texture that we remember! "

4 slices bacon, diced
1 large onion, finely chopped
2 cans (16 ounces each)
    baked beans
1 cup ketchup
1/3 cup molasses (see below)
1/4 cup butter, cut into small pieces
2 tablespoons yellow mustard

1 Spread the bacon and onion evenly over the bottom of a microwave-safe 9" x 13" baking dish. Cover with a paper towel and microwave at 80% power for 5 minutes.

2 Add the remaining ingredients; mix well then cover and microwave at 80% power for 13 minutes, stirring halfway through the cooking time.

DID YOU KNOW...

that there's a no-fuss way to measure molasses? Simply coat the measuring cup or spoon with vegetable oil then pour and measure away! The molasses will slide right off the surface of whatever you're measuring in/with, instead of clinging to it and making for tough cleanup.

Cheesy Baked Pineapple

9 to 12 servings

" If you've never tried this dynamite duo, you're in for a big surprise! This tropical flavor combination is a nice change of pace that your gang won't be able to pass up. "

2 cans (20 ounces each)
    pineapple chunks, drained
2 cups (8 ounces) shredded sharp
    Cheddar cheese
1/2 cup sugar
3 tablespoons all-purpose flour
1/4 cup (1/2 stick) butter, melted
2 cups coarsely crushed butter-
    flavored crackers

1 Coat a microwave-safe 9" x 13" baking dish with nonstick cooking spray. Place the pineapple in the baking dish.

2 In a medium bowl, combine the cheese, sugar, and flour; mix well then sprinkle evenly over the pineapple. Microwave at 70% power for 6 minutes, or until the cheese melts.

3 Drizzle butter over the top then sprinkle with the crushed crackers. Microwave at 70% power for 1 minute, or until heated through.

Cinnamon Apple Rings

4 to 6 servings

" Love the smell and taste of baked apples fresh from the oven? Well, now it'll take you no time to whip up these juicy, sweet baked apples for dinner. There's nothing better than this down-home country taste! "

1/4 cup (1/2 stick) butter
4 Granny Smith apples, cored
    and cut into 1/4-inch rings
1/3 cup packed light brown sugar
1 teaspoon ground cinnamon

1 In a microwave-safe 9" x 13" baking dish, heat the butter at 80% power for 1 to 1-1/2 minutes, until melted. Add the apple rings, turning until well coated. Microwave at 80% power for 10 minutes, stirring halfway through the cooking time.

2 In a small bowl, combine the brown sugar and cinnamon; mix well then sprinkle over the apples.

3 Microwave at 80% power for 1 to 2 minutes, or until the brown sugar dissolves into the butter. Serve immediately.

DID YOU KNOW...

that you can use the microwave to take the chill off fruit stored in the refrigerator? If you store apples and similar types of fruit in the refrigerator, all you have to do is place it on a microwave-safe plate and heat for about 1 minute at 50% power. Besides softening the fruit, it'll bring out loads of flavor!

Desserts

Pineapple Upside-Down Cake
12 to 14 servings

" If you asked me to recommend just one recipe from this book, it would have to be this one. Why? 'Cause the advanced technology of the Panasonic Inverter microwave turns out a spectacular version of this traditional thermal oven recipe! "

2/3 cup packed light brown sugar

4 tablespoons (1/2 stick) butter, cut into small pieces

1 can (20 ounces) pineapple rings, drained

7 to 10 maraschino cherries

1 package (18.25 ounces) yellow cake mix

1 cup water

1/4 cup vegetable oil

3 eggs

DID YOU KNOW...

that cakes continue to cook even after removal from the oven or microwave? That means we have to be sure that the cake still looks and feels a bit moist before taking it out to cool.

Photo Page 2

1 Sprinkle the brown sugar over the bottom of a microwave-safe 10-inch round cake pan or 9" x 13" baking dish; dot with butter. Microwave at 100% power for 1-1/2 minutes. Stir to distribute the mixture evenly over the bottom of the pan; top with pineapple rings arranged in a single layer then place a cherry in each ring.

2 In a large bowl, combine the cake mix, water, oil, and eggs. Beat until well mixed. Spoon the batter into the pan and microwave at 70% power for 14 minutes, or until cooked through.

3 Let the cake stand for about 5 minutes. Loosen gently with a knife and invert onto a platter. Serve warm, or allow to cool completely before serving.

Homestyle Chocolate Cake Mix
About 6-1/2 cups

" Did you ever think of saving time and money by making your own cake mix? It makes sense to mix up a batch of this and keep it on hand for making any of a bunch of chocolate goodies. And the next time you're in the baking mood, there are options on the next page for yummy treats you can bake up in no time with this simple homemade mix! "

3 cups sugar
2 cups all-purpose flour
2 cups unsweetened cocoa
1-1/2 teaspoons baking powder

1 Combine all the ingredients in a large resealable plastic bag; seal the bag then shake until the ingredients are thoroughly combined.

2 Store mix in the sealed plastic bag, or in a tightly covered container. Shake or mix well before using in the recipes on the following page.

FINISHING TOUCH:

When making Chocolate Cake Squares or Express Chocolate Cupcakes (opposite page) using this mix, all you have to do to make them look really fancy is to add a dusting of confectioners' sugar just before serving, or top with prepared or homemade frosting when cooled.

Desserts

Chocolate Cake Squares
About 9 servings

" Whether it's for a children's birthday party or an everyday treat for the gang, these homestyle desserts will certainly take the cake! "

2 cups Homestyle Chocolate Cake
   Mix (recipe at left)
2 eggs
1/2 cup mayonnaise
1/2 cup milk

1 Coat a microwave-safe 8-inch square baking dish with nonstick cooking spray. In a large bowl, combine all the ingredients; stir until well combined then pour into the baking dish.

2 Microwave at 70% power for 6 minutes, or until a wooden toothpick inserted in the center comes out clean. Let cool, then cut into squares, and serve.

Express Chocolate Cupcakes
6 cupcakes

1 cup Homestyle Chocolate Cake
   Mix (recipe at left)
1 egg
1/4 cup mayonnaise
1/4 cup milk

1 Place 6 paper baking cups in a microwave-safe muffin pan, or side by side in a microwave-safe 7" x 11" baking dish.

2 In a medium bowl, combine all the ingredients; stir until well combined then spoon evenly into the baking cups.

3 Microwave at 80% power for 3 minutes, or until a wooden toothpick inserted in the center comes out clean. Let cool, then serve.

Rocky Road Cake
12 to 15 servings

" Gone are the days of standing watch over our chocolate and marshmallow creme as it melts. Thanks to the even heat distribution provided by Inverter technology, we can be sure of getting silky smooth melted results every time. "

1 package (18.25 ounces) chocolate cake mix, batter prepared according to package directions
1/2 cup plus 2 tablespoons mini semisweet chocolate chips, divided
1/2 cup plus 2 tablespoons chopped walnuts, divided
1 cup marshmallow creme

1 Coat a microwave-safe 9" x 13" baking dish with nonstick cooking spray.

2 Add 1/2 cup chocolate chips and 1/2 cup walnuts to the cake batter; mix well then pour into the baking dish. Microwave at 80% power for 12 to 13 minutes, or until a wooden toothpick inserted in the center comes out clean. Remove from the microwave and let cool.

3 In a medium-sized microwave-safe bowl, microwave the marshmallow creme at 70% power for 1 to 2 minutes, stirring every 10 seconds until melted. Pour over the cake then sprinkle with the remaining 2 tablespoons each of chocolate chips and walnuts. Cut into squares and serve.

DID YOU KNOW...

that the Panasonic Inverter microwave allows you to manually choose the required power level? Simply press the "Power Level" key pad until the desired power appears in the display window, enter the cooking time then press "Start."

Photo Page 38

Desserts

Peanut Butter and Jelly Bars
15 to 18 bars

" Did somebody say that our favorite combo of peanut butter and jelly is just for sandwiches? Uh uh! This lunchtime favorite is now a fun dessert that can be ready in just 10 minutes! "

2-1/4 cups all-purpose flour
1/2 cup (1 stick) butter, melted
1/2 cup creamy peanut butter
1/2 cup packed light brown sugar
1 egg
1 cup strawberry jelly, jam or
    preserves

1 In a large bowl, combine all the ingredients except the jelly. Beat with an electric beater on medium speed for 2 minutes, or until blended and crumbly; set aside 1 cup of the mixture.

2 Spread the remaining mixture over the bottom of a microwave-safe 9" x 13" baking dish. Spread the jelly evenly over the top and crumble the reserved peanut butter mixture over the top.

3 Microwave at 70% power for 6 minutes. Allow to cool then cut into bars.

DID YOU KNOW...

that you can use your Inverter microwave for melting peanut butter? It comes in handy when you're making recipes that call for peanut butter to be swirled through cakes and brownies, and also when you just want to make it easier to spread.

Photo Page 4

Pecan Toffee Bars

15 to 18 bars

> In need of a fun, new after-dinner delight? Team this with fresh coffee for a grand finale fit for any meal!

2 cups all-purpose flour
1/2 cup (1 stick) butter, softened
1 can (14 ounces) sweetened
    condensed milk
1 egg
1 teaspoon vanilla extract
1 cup chopped pecans
1-1/2 cups toffee chips

1 Coat a microwave-safe 9" x 13" baking dish with nonstick cooking spray.

2 In a large bowl, combine the flour and butter until crumbly. Press evenly over the bottom of the baking dish. Microwave at 70% power for 3 minutes.

3 In a medium bowl, combine the remaining ingredients; mix well and spread evenly over the crust, covering the surface completely.

4 Microwave at 70% power for 6 minutes, until bubbly. Allow to cool completely then cut into bars and serve.

FINISHING TOUCH:

Sprinkle 1 cup semisweet chocolate chips over the top immediately after removing the dish from the microwave for an extra wow!

Raspberry Brownies

12 wedges

" Was there ever a more decadent flavor combination than chocolate and raspberry? I doubt I could find one in a quick dessert that satisfies like these rich brownies. **"**

1 package (21 to 23 ounces) brownie mix, batter prepared according to the package directions
3/4 cup semisweet chocolate chips
3/4 cup raspberry preserves, divided

1 Coat a microwave-safe 9-inch deep-dish pie plate with nonstick cooking spray.

2 Add the chocolate chips and 1/2 cup raspberry preserves to the brownie batter; mix well then pour into the pie plate.

3 Microwave at 80% power for 9 minutes, or until a wooden toothpick inserted in the center comes out clean. Remove from the microwave and let cool.

4 Spread the remaining 1/4 cup preserves over the brownies. Cut into wedges, and serve.

FINISHING TOUCH:

Take this treat over the top by serving each wedge crowned with a scoop of ice cream and some fresh raspberries. Mmm mmm!

Crispy Tiger Fudge

About 3 dozen squares

❝ Want to let somebody know he or she is special to you? Just whip this up, wrap a few pieces in colorful plastic wrap, and tie with a ribbon. Believe me, your gift from the heart will go a long way! ❞

2 packages (6 ounces each) white baking bars
1/3 cup creamy peanut butter
1 cup crispy rice cereal
1 cup (6 ounces) semisweet chocolate chips

1 In a large microwave-safe bowl, melt the white baking bars and peanut butter at 70% power for 2-1/2 minutes, stirring at 30-second intervals until melted and well combined.

2 Stir in the cereal until thoroughly coated; spread into an 8-inch square baking dish.

3 In a medium-sized microwave-safe bowl, melt the chocolate chips at 70% power for 2 to 2-1/2 minutes, stirring at 30-second intervals until melted.

4 Spread the melted chocolate over the cereal layer until completely covered. Chill for about 1 hour, or until firm. Cut into squares and serve.

DID YOU KNOW...

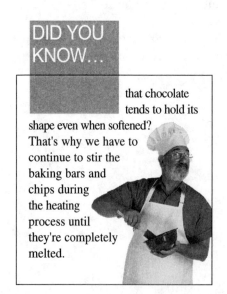

that chocolate tends to hold its shape even when softened? That's why we have to continue to stir the baking bars and chips during the heating process until they're completely melted.

Chocolate Almond Truffles
2 dozen truffles

" We don't need a full-service bakery to churn out these little goodies! With an Inverter microwave, making homemade truffles was never so easy! "

1 cup (1/2 pint) heavy cream
6 tablespoons butter, cut up
1 package (12 ounces) semisweet
    chocolate chips
2 cups confectioners' sugar
1 teaspoon almond extract
1-1/2 cups sliced blanched
    almonds, chopped

1 In a large microwave-safe bowl, combine the heavy cream and butter; microwave at 80% power for 2 minutes. Add the chocolate chips, stir, and microwave at 80% power for 30 seconds, stirring halfway through heating.

2 Add the confectioners' sugar and almond extract; stir until well combined. Cover and chill for 2 hours, or until firm enough to form into balls.

3 Place the almonds in a shallow dish. Form the chocolate mixture into 24 one-inch balls and roll the balls in the almonds, covering completely. Place on a platter, cover, and chill for 1 hour, or until firm.

UNLIMITED OPTIONS:

These make great gifts for a special occasion or any time you want to make someone's day. Simply place a few truffles in a gift tin or box, surround with festive tissue paper, and get ready to share the smiles!

Blueberry Clusters

About 2 dozen

" This unique anytime treat gets the award for 'Quickest Party Favorite.' So, the next time you're in need of a 'gotta have it now' snack, this is your winner! "

1 tablespoon vegetable shortening
1 package (6 ounces) white baking
    bars, coarsely chopped
1 pint fresh blueberries, rinsed
    and dried

1 In a medium-sized microwave-safe bowl, combine the vegetable shortening and chopped baking bars.

2 Microwave at 30% power for 2 minutes; stir. Microwave at 30% power for 1 minute; stir until melted and smooth. Add the blueberries, stirring until well coated.

3 Drop the mixture by heaping teaspoonfuls onto a waxed paper-lined cookie sheet. Chill for 30 minutes, or until firm. Serve, or transfer to an airtight container and keep chilled until ready to serve.

UNLIMITED OPTIONS:

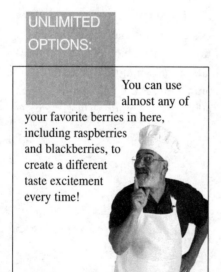

You can use almost any of your favorite berries in here, including raspberries and blackberries, to create a different taste excitement every time!

Desserts

Crustless Cheesecake Pie

8 to 10 servings

❝ Love the taste of soft and creamy cheesecake, but hate to spend hours in the kitchen making it? Here's a delectable Inverter microwave cheesecake that tastes oven-baked yet keeps our kitchens cool! ❞

2 packages (8 ounces each) cream cheese, softened
2/3 cup plus 3 tablespoons sugar, divided
3 eggs
1-1/2 teaspoons vanilla extract, divided
1/2 teaspoon fresh lemon juice, divided
1 container (16 ounces) sour cream

FINISHING TOUCH:

Wanna turn this into an eye-catching classic? Simply spread a can of cherry pie filling over the top once the pie has cooled.

1 Coat a microwave-safe 9-inch deep-dish pie plate with nonstick cooking spray.

2 In a large bowl, with an electric beater on medium speed, beat the cream cheese and 2/3 cup sugar until smooth. Beat in the eggs one at a time then beat in 1/2 teaspoon vanilla and 1/4 teaspoon lemon juice; pour into the pie plate.

3 Microwave at 70% power for 7 minutes. Remove from the microwave and let sit for about 5 minutes.

4 In a medium bowl, combine the sour cream and the remaining 3 tablespoons sugar, 1 teaspoon vanilla, and 1/4 teaspoon lemon juice; mix well then pour over the top of the pie.

5 Microwave at 70% power for 3 minutes. Let cool then cover and chill for at least 4 hours before serving.

Candy Apple Tarts

6 servings

" Who doesn't love the taste of ruby red, candy-coated apples? When we wanna 'wow' our gang with a different dessert, this one captures the tastes we remember…and is sure to make us the apple of their eyes! "

1 cup apple juice
2 tablespoons cornstarch
1/3 cup red-hot cinnamon candies
1/2 teaspoon vanilla extract
1/4 teaspoon red food color
4 tart cooking apples, peeled, cored, and thinly sliced
6 single-serve graham cracker crusts

1 In a large microwave-safe bowl, combine the apple juice, cornstarch, cinnamon candies, vanilla, and food color; mix well.

2 Stir in the apples then microwave at 70% power for 12 minutes, or until the apples are tender; mix well.

3 Spoon equal amounts of the apple mixture into the crusts. Cover loosely and chill for at least 1 hour before serving.

FINISHING TOUCH:

These look great when you top each one with a dollop of whipped cream and a few additional cinnamon candies just before serving.

Quick Homemade Flan
12 to 16 servings

" Want a restaurant-style favorite without leaving home? Well, now we can make this caramel custard goodie easier than ever! "

1 cup sugar
4 teaspoons water
1 teaspoon lemon juice
1 can (12 ounces) evaporated milk
1 can (14 ounces) sweetened
    condensed milk
6 eggs
2 teaspoons vanilla extract

1 Coat a microwave-safe 8-inch square baking dish with nonstick cooking spray. Sprinkle the sugar over the bottom of the dish; drizzle with the water and lemon juice.

2 Microwave at 70% power for 5 to 6 minutes, or until the sugar dissolves and starts to brown; set aside to cool.

3 In a blender, combine the evaporated and sweetened condensed milks, the eggs, and vanilla until well combined. Pour over the caramelized sugar mixture; cover and microwave at 80% power for 7 minutes.

4 Let cool then cover and chill for at least 4 hours. Just before serving, gently loosen the flan from the edge of the dish with a knife and invert onto a serving platter.

DID YOU KNOW...

...that heating an item containing metal in the microwave oven can cause mini fireworks? This includes baking dishes, utensils, aluminum pans and foil, and even certain decorated paper plates! In simple terms, the microwaves bounce off metal and can actually damage the walls of the oven. If you notice that your oven starts sparking, turn it off immediately.

White–Chocolate Mint Mousse
6 to 8 servings

" In need of a light and refreshing dessert? I've got a cool idea for giving ordinary mousse a minty makeover! "

1 package (6 ounces) white baking
    bars, broken up
2 cups (1 pint) heavy cream,
    divided
1-1/2 teaspoons mint extract
1/3 cup confectioners' sugar
8 drops green food color

1 In a medium-sized microwave-safe bowl, combine the baking bars and 1/2 cup heavy cream. Microwave at 40% power for 2 to 3 minutes, stirring every 30 seconds. Remove the bowl from the microwave and stir until the mixture is well combined and smooth.

2 Stir in the mint extract, confectioners' sugar, and food color; mix well then let cool.

3 In a large bowl, beat the remaining 1-1/2 cups heavy cream until stiff peaks form. Gently fold in the cooled mint mixture until well blended.

4 Cover and chill for at least 1 hour before serving.

Desserts

Very Chocolate Fondue
About 1-1/2 cups

" Ever wonder how to make that fancy restaurant-style silky smooth chocolate fondue that's always a big dessert hit? Well, even if you don't have a fondue pot, you can still recreate this romantic favorite at home! "

2 squares (1 ounce each)
    unsweetened chocolate
1 can (14 ounces) sweetened
    condensed milk
1/3 cup mini marshmallows
1 teaspoon instant coffee granules
1 teaspoon hot water

1 In a medium-sized microwave-safe bowl, combine the chocolate, sweetened condensed milk, and marshmallows. Microwave at 70% power for 2 to 3 minutes, stirring every 20 seconds until the chocolate and marshmallows melt and are smooth and well combined.

2 In a small bowl, dissolve the coffee granules in the hot water. Add to the chocolate mixture; mix well. Serve immediately.

UNLIMITED OPTIONS:

Serve this with your favorite fresh fruit, pound cake marshmallows, squares, and other decadent dippers.

Nutty Sundae Cones

12 servings

" Remember how all the kids in the neighborhood would run home for change when the ice cream truck came by ringing its bell? I've got an easy way to make those all-time favorite sundae cones we all would choose from the truck! **"**

1 cup chopped salted peanuts, divided
12 five-ounce paper cups
1 cup (6 ounces) semisweet chocolate chips
2 tablespoons vegetable shortening
1 quart vanilla ice cream
12 sugar cones

1 Place 1 teaspoon peanuts into each paper cup. In a medium-sized microwave-safe bowl, microwave the chocolate chips and shortening at 90% power for 1 minute; stir until smooth and completely melted. Microwave at additional 10-second intervals, if necessary.

2 Stir the remaining peanuts into the melted chocolate. Spoon about 2 teaspoons of the mixture into each cup, or enough for the mixture to coat halfway up the sides of each cup.

3 One at a time, place a scoop of vanilla ice cream into each cone, and invert the cones into the cups, pressing the ice cream into the chocolate mixture. Freeze the cones in the cups for 3 to 4 hours. When ready to serve, simply peel off the paper cups.

DID YOU KNOW...

that we can soften hard-to-scoop ice cream in our Inverter microwaves? Just heat the ice cream at 20% power for about 30 seconds, making sure to check it frequently so it doesn't turn into ice cream soup!

Desserts

Peach Melba Parfaits

6 to 8 servings

" This classic dessert is pretty to look at, and oh-so-satisfying to dig into. Your family won't be able to resist the juicy peaches and colorful berries! "

1 can (29 ounces) peach halves, drained and chopped
4 tablespoons (1/2 stick) butter, thinly sliced
6 tablespoons light brown sugar
1 tablespoon peach schnapps (optional)
1 quart vanilla ice cream
1 cup whipped cream
1/2 pint fresh raspberries
1 bunch fresh mint (optional)

1 Place the peaches, butter, and brown sugar in a microwave-safe 8-inch square baking dish. Microwave at 100% power for 3 minutes. Stir in the schnapps, if desired.

2 Scoop the ice cream evenly into individual serving bowls or parfait glasses then spoon the peach mixture over the top.

3 Dollop with whipped cream and garnish with fresh raspberries and mint sprigs, if desired.

DID YOU KNOW...

that peach melba was originally created by the renowned French chef Auguste Escoffier in the late 1800s in honor of popular Australian opera singer Dame Nellie Melba? I guess that means we can call this one a true masterpiece!

Photo Page 39

Chocolate Peanut Butter Pops
6 pops

" If you need an excuse to get the kids excited about cooking, here it is! These pops are easy to make and give us a fun way to spend time in the kitchen with the kids. "

1/3 cup sugar
1/4 cup unsweetened cocoa
2 tablespoons cornstarch
1-1/2 cups milk
1/4 cup creamy peanut butter
6 five-ounce paper cups
6 non-toxic craft sticks

1 In a medium-sized microwave-safe bowl, combine the sugar, cocoa, and cornstarch; mix well.

2 Whisk in the milk then microwave at 60% power for 2 minutes. Whisk again then microwave at 60% power for 3 minutes, or until mixture is thickened. Whisk in the peanut butter until well combined.

3 Spoon the mixture equally into the paper cups. Place a craft stick in the center of each cup and freeze until firm.

4 To serve, remove the cups from the freezer and let sit for a few minutes, or simply peel off the paper cups and enjoy.

Desserts

Peanut Butter Cup Roll-Ups

4 roll-ups

Here's a sweet and creamy dessert that's easy to make when we're short on time but don't want to get caught short on taste!

3/4 cup creamy peanut butter
Four 10-inch flour tortillas
1/2 cup mini semisweet chocolate
    chips

1 Spread the peanut butter over the tortillas then sprinkle evenly with the chocolate chips. Roll up tightly jelly-roll style.

2 Wrap each roll-up in a sheet of waxed paper, twisting the ends to seal. Microwave for 10 to 15 seconds, or until the chocolate chips are melted. Serve immediately.